Surviving Five Daughters

by
LYNN JACOBSON

ISBN: 1-4392-0799-2
ISBN-13: 9781439207994

Visit www.booksurge.com to order additional copies.

To my five incredibly beautiful daughters,
Julie, Lisa, Mandy, Tienlyn and Raelyn
and my most wonderful, beautiful wife, Meimei.

They have given me so much more than I ever
expected and certainly far more than I deserved.

TABLE OF CONTENTS

ILLUSTRATIONS

PREFACE

Like most males of my generation, I married too young. The union didn't last so at thirty-one, I returned to graduate school in Colorado as a single father caring for three daughters. In those days it was difficult for a single mother to find a job and apartment leading to the agreement that I would take the girls for the first two years until their mother got settled.

Five years later, I was smitten and followed my true love to California so she could earn her MBA. After seventeen unsuccessful attempts to convince her to marry me, I went over her head and asked her mother for permission to marry her daughter. Not daring to disobey her mother, MFG (my favorite girlfriend) became MFW (my favorite wife). Five years later, MFW informed me, "The doctor said we're set to have an all girls basketball team." Poof! Five daughters.

While sharing with the reader the agonies, rewards and survival techniques of raising five daughters, I refer to my daughters as D1 through D5 to save ink and to save them the embarrassment of having to admit I'm their father.

Major Contributors Deserving Recognition

Tienlyn Jacobson wrote the second half of all six Panther Track chapters.

Meimei Pan (My Favorite Wife) drew all the cartoons.

Raelyn and Lynn Jacobson jointly designed the cover.

Meimei Pan and Raelyn Jacobson performed major editing.

Angie Eagan, Richard Graglia, Stephanie Nerres and other good friends were helpful readers.

Julie Savage, Lisa Rice, Mandy Hartman, Tienlyn Jacobson, Raelyn Jacobson and Meimei Pan provided all the material – I only had to write it down.

Mandatory skill for all new fathers: one-hand typing.

Two fathers meet.
"I have an excessive number of daughters!"
"What a coincidence. I have far too many, too!"
"I have five. How many do you have?"
"One."
"Is she thirteen by any chance?"
"Why, yes. How did you know?"

1

It's a Girl.
It's a Girl.
It's a Girl.
It's a Girl!
It's a Girl!!
or

RIDING THE ESTROGEN TSUNAMI

Fathers with daughters focus on the "Six Ws of daughter raising" learned through frontline in-the-trenches battle experience, as opposed to the "Five Ws of the reporting profession" taught in journalism school. The six Ws that entangle fathers are: Wonder (pregnancy), Wow (birth), Wee (ages two to twelve), Wait (ages thirteen to seventeen), Whew (daughter finally turns eighteen) and Whoopee (age thirty-six) when they are actually off the payroll. An overlay of "whelmed" (as in "overwhelmed") and "weep" when they are born, enter kindergarten, get hurt, leave for college, graduate, get married, have their own babies and forget to call round out this whole

Daughter Wonderment thing. Perhaps this book should have been titled, "Weep, Wonder, and Wejoice."

I was taking my youngest daughter, then eight, for her third ski outing in Colorado. After a few warm-up runs on a beginner slope I felt she was ready to tackle one of the easier intermediate slopes.

We got off the intermediate lift for our first run around 10:00 a.m., discussed our plan, and then I led off first and pulled up twenty yards down-slope to watch her progress.

"Wait for me, Daddy. Wait for me!"

After ten minutes of gingerly negotiating the bumps and ending up on her butt a few times, she joined me and we discussed her progress. I then skied down another twenty yards and again watched her ski to me.

"Wait for me, Daddy! Wait for me!

For the next hour and a half we repeated this scenario gradually extending the distances between stops to a hundred yards by the time we reached the lift.

Fast forward to 3:30 p.m. Off the lift and down the slope. This time I skied as fast as my out-of-shape body would tolerate, stopping only when it screamed for mercy. I reached the lift at 3:50 p.m. only to see my daughter with both hands on her hips.

"Where have you been?" she demanded. "I've been waiting for you for at least five minutes!"

This summarizes my whole world of raising daughters. It started with, **"Wait for me!"** and somewhere along the way progresses to, **"Where have you been?"**

RAISING FIVE DAUGHTERS

My experience of raising five daughters can best be compared to an intense nonstop sporting event — but with three opposing sides vying for an advantage instead of two. These three sides are identified as follows:

1) Offense: the mother, grandmother, godmother, other female members of the extended family, and an occasional unknown woman just passing by who feels compelled to voice her opinion although she is in the picture for under twenty seconds—all intent on giving "constructive" advice.

2) Defense: the daughter, her siblings (when it is to their advantage to be on the same side, i.e., common enemy), plus her peer group (backed up by an extensive phone/ Internet network), who are just trying to make it through one more day negotiating the treacherous minefields of estrogen driven teenage-hood,

and

3) Nonsense: the father, who, though extensively involved, is oblivious to the intricacies and subtleties of the constantly changing rules non-rules and who watches the game intently from somewhere out in left field (rooting for everyone of course) in a playing area that doesn't seem to have a left field.

Although understanding that the rules are out of reach for the typical father (being a mere mortal), it is my hope the following chapters will provide some insight to those fathers who may venture down a similar slippery but rewarding path and let them know others have actually survived the challenge. Good luck and may the force be with you—you will need it. How does that expression go? When it comes to raising daughters, "We not only believe in miracles; we rely on them!"

2

ESTROGEN TSUNAMI

Five daughters (D1 through D5), my favorite wife (MFW), and my favorite mother-in-law (MFM) give me an overall domestic E/T ratio (Estrogen/Testosterone ratio) equal to 7, a full three standard deviations above the norm of 1. We once had a male cat named Marshmallow but, as he had been fixed (not my idea), he was unable to contribute to my side of this ratio. Fuzzball, our rabbit, a dumb bunny of uncertain gender, was also of no help.

This E/T ratio should not be confused with either *E.T.*, *the Extra-Terrestrial* or the TV program *ET, Entertainment Tonight,* even though the environment in our house is both "other worldly" and to non-males, greatly entertaining. Some use this E/T value as a metric for measuring the magnitude of the Estrogen Tsunami in any daughter-laden household.

This abnormally high ratio has an enormous impact on my approach to life's little decisions. For example, after years of buying secondhand cars, we finally sprang for a top-of-the-line minivan. Within days I disabled the audio portion of the GPS directional system which featured a woman's voice giving me commands. I just couldn't handle one more female telling me what to do—frankly, I'd rather risk getting lost.

Just as there are special exemptions that permit certain fuel-efficient cars with a single occupant to drive in commuter lanes, I fervently believe that anyone with an E/T over 5 should be, at a minimum, entitled to park in handicapped parking.

I avoid golf not only because I'm overbooked with so many attention-demanding women in my life but also because I'm fearful of what my response might be should someone ask, "So tell me, what is your handicap?"

"Are you kidding? With five daughters..."

On the rare occasion when I have run into another father of five daughters (met one with six once; poor soul, spent a lot of time talking to himself and staring into the distance, obviously a case of severe Post Daughter Stress Syndrome, PDSS), we could always agree on one thing: it's virtually impossible to explain to the other 99.6 percent of the near-normal world what it's like living in such an estrogen-saturated environment. The challenge is not unlike trying to describe to someone the experience of riding a camel when all they've ever ridden are horses.

I do admit that I whip out my ever-present group photo of the fabulous five when given even the slightest opportunity. Every viewer is totally taken by the high density of beauty in my photo, and several young men have eagerly inquired as to each daughter's marital status. More then once I've had to be assertive to retrieve the photo from the clutches of a smitten soul.

As often as not, a typical viewer holds the photo up close to his or her face in both hands studying its every detail. Then they stare at me with a puzzled look. Finally following a long pause, during which time you can sense their internal struggle between "need for clarification" and "social etiquette," they involuntarily blurt out, "So, so tell me, if you don't mind. Who's the father?"

Is it difficult being the father to five such beauties? No, not difficult at all but one is very busy. I mean really, really busy. As MFW would explain to acquaintances, "If I could just get him to slow down, I am sure he could learn to become a type A personality."

With five daughters, a father's survival is premised on humor, patience, some smarts, skill at looking under rocks for money, humor, more than his share of dumb luck, an understanding that employing logic under such circumstances has limited value, humor, and, most importantly of all, knowing when to invoke strategic surrender. Of course, I must confess that despite my outward kvetching, when five daughters have such an overabundance of love as mine do, life can hardly get any better.

Friends have suggested that to ease my sense of being overwhelmed, I should try meditation (or was that medication?) I enrolled in a meditation class once but even after several months of practice it didn't seem to help. Frankly it made me more nervous. I don't understand why—I tried to meditate as fast as I could. I'm now trying to locate a good levitation class to see if it could at least bring a bit more levity into my life.

Although I refer to my daughters as D1, D2, D3... throughout this book, a close friend, aware of their ability to drain my resources, has suggested I refer to them instead as P1, P2, P3 ...where P stands for Poverty.

*I saw nothing wrong with my daughters' wishing
to be better off than us until I realized that a
major part of their plan included a serious attack
on our assets.*

3

PENTE-DAUGHTERED FATHERS

Although dictionaries are wonderful innovations, some words never make the cut for dictionary inclusion because their use meanders just under the utilitarian-horizon.

A new word, coined on the fly, might be understood in context even though it may have a half-life of less than three seconds. For example, most people would understand: "Get your wicky-wicky over here!" New words eventually either percolate above the fuzzy boundary for dictionary inclusion or fade into oblivion due to lack of interest.

That said, I believe that if "five-daughters" were a noun, it would fail to make the cut as only fathers of five daughters could possibly grasp its full ramifications. Everyone else would be left totally clueless. So even though I'd love to coin the noun, "pente-daughtered father" or PDF, until someone can suggest a word that has a better chance of sticking around, I'm not optimistic about its chances for survival.

PDFs unite. We have nothing to lose except our identity as "estrogenically-overwhelmed testosteronically-challenged" males.

For many years, when asked about the number and gender distribution of my children, I would respond in a glib fashion, mildly complaining about the overwhelming estrogen levels created by so many (albeit beautiful, intelligent, charming, loving...) females in my life. More recently, I have found it prudent to revert back to answering with a simple, "five daughters," after discovering that several fathers I've encountered begin to shake uncontrollably at the mere prospect of having even a third daughter added to their household, much less a fourth or fifth daughter.

All things are relative except, of course, when it concerns daughters, where on more than one occasion we thought how nice it would be if they were actually someone else's relatives.

When I mentioned to a Vietnamese woman that I had "five daughters" she responded, "Oh, you are so fortunate! In my country, having five daughters is considered very good luck. Five sons; no. Five daughters; yes."

In the U.S., when I told another PDF about this Vietnamese woman's encouraging response, he quipped, "Yeah sure. But that saying was invented in Southeast Asia at least a thousand years ago, well before it became common to mention college tuitions and bankruptcy in the same breath."

My PDF status was a subject of great amusement to Mary, a street vendor, and her friends while we were exploring the side markets in the Bahamas. Mary pulled MFW over and in a very serious tone, admonished her, "Five daughters and no sons? You must make your man eat conch (a mollusk eaten in the Bahamas). Only conch will make sons." (So how do sons get made in Iowa? Perhaps corn on the cob is a suitable substitute?) Everyone has an opinion when encountering a family seemingly lopsided with girls.

I find I am in a subcategory of PDFs. Whereas most PDFs achieve their "involuntary" status as a result of their effort to keep trying until they produce a son, I'm a PDF who never gave that motivation a second thought. I really like having daughters and am not really sure how I'd actually go about trying to raise a son.

If you want to get an involuntary laugh from any father of girls, but especially from a PDF, try approaching him with, "So, tell me, just so I'll know for future reference, at what age do daughters start sending money home?"

I mentioned to D4: "Daughter, I just did the numbers. Instead of sending you to a private girls' school for three years and then onto a private college, we could have used those funds to purchase three houses for you in Grand Junction, Colorado— all for cash. You could have then rented two of the houses and taken on a roommate in the third, keeping two bedrooms for yourself. You could have retired at eighteen!"

D4 stared at me intently for a long, long time. I could see an expression of total disbelief on her face. Then, finally she responded in a very slow measured voice.

"Great. Just great. Now you tell me?"

I brought the five Ds together for a family meeting and explained to them that there were some very serious family issues that strongly needed addressing.

"As the five of you know, several years ago I used to have ten daughters. After careful evaluation, I decided to keep the best five. Now, due to our deteriorating financial situation and exploding chaos, I'm considering cutting back to four so I strongly suggest you SHAPE UP!"

This startling (at least I thought so) announcement had no effect. Sometimes it's really hard for a PDF to get any attention, much less respect from five daughters. When the five of them are together, the communication interchange is so intense that all non-daughter-to-daughter data ports are either usurped or shut down altogether.

*Advice: When your daughter moves out for the
third time, quickly rent out your home, move into
a 400 sq. ft. condo with a single parking space and
happily inform her, "You can come stay with us
any time you want."*

4
CHECKOUT TIME

Parents are convinced that the primary objective of every fourteen-year-old daughter is to subject them to as much anxiety as possible. Likewise, every fourteen-year-old daughter is equally convinced that the primary objective of her parents is to embarrass her to the fullest extent possible, especially in front of her friends. Turns out, particularly in these endeavors, we are a family of overachievers.

I have concluded from both my observations and from consultations with other parents that the highest status a middle school daughter thinks she can achieve in the eyes of her peers is for her to be an orphan, thus escaping the clearly dumb things that her parents do to totally mess up her social life.

Fortunately somewhere around tenth grade, they come to the conclusion that the benefits of having parents actually outweigh the benefits of being an orphan. I suspect a gradually increasing awareness of the parents' non-minor role in their financial well-being (e.g., gas money, clothes, fast food, makeup, cell phones, cash, etc.) may be at play here. They also acknowledge that parents provide support services (e.g., laundry, wake-up calls, cable, online access, and a fully stocked refrigerator for them and their friends). Still, many of the parents' roles such as covering for them during awkward situations (e.g., parent answers phone, discovers would-be love interest on the line, covers mouthpiece, "What should I tell him?" "Tell him I'm not here.") remain unacknowledged.

Nonetheless, this change of heart gives me great comfort when, according to the popular joke going around (at least I hope it's a joke—please tell me it's a joke!), it is these same kids who will pick our nursing home.

I have noticed a renewed interest for parents of teenage daughters to mount a large in-your-face sign over the couch in the family room that announces:

A friendly reminder from the management

CHECKOUT FROM THIS FACILITY IS Age 18

At Noon*

*A one-hour courtesy-delay in checkout time may be granted for good behavior at management's discretion. Cleaning/fumigation charges may be imposed following room inspection. Items left unclaimed for thirty days will be removed following normal hazardous waste disposal procedures.

This may come as a surprise but you do not get
an A for bragging: "Hey, ninety-seven percent of
the time in the shower, I did not drop the baby."

5

How to Give Baby a Shower

The first three rules for giving your baby a shower are:

Rule 1) Don't drop the baby.

Rule 2) Don't drop the baby.

Rule 3) Don't drop the baby.

And, of course, when in doubt see Rule 1.

Not dropping the baby means not losing your concentration and keeping a good hold on her at all times. During all position transitions, it is important to maintain good friction between you and the baby, which means creating a no-slip zone.

Soap is death to friction so don't let soap get between the two of you on any part of your bodies where you might need friction for support. I never released my hold on a daughter's leg with my left hand during shower time, thus assuring no soap could "do its thing" in loosening my grip. When we were visiting other parts of the country that had very soft water, I often found it difficult to remove the slippery effects of soap from our bodies. In these situations I found I could retain a good portion of the needed friction by wearing a T-shirt during our shower time.

For those fathers adorned with an abundance of body hair, wearing a T-shirt has an additional benefit: the baby is less able to support herself by clinging to your chest hair (yikes), a problem I've not seen properly addressed in baby books.

My preferred technique was to cradle her in my left arm with a firm grip of her left thigh. I kept her right hip pressed in on my left hip, also soap free. This left my right hand to do all the washing. Don't forget to wash between the toes and in the creases between her tummy (we have stomachs; babies have tummies) and thighs. Keep rinsing often to prevent soap buildup.

Keeping one's concentration does not preclude singing to your baby during your shower. If ever you had a captive audience, this is it, and, since she is not yet able to voice her opinion on the quality of your arias, you can pretend you are in top form. As often as not, she will make an effort to join you in a duet. I discovered that, as often as not, one of us was flat.

A crucial thing to remember is that what is lukewarm to an adult may be hot to a baby. One bad memory I have of my childhood is burning my hands in water my mother insisted was not too hot. So keep the temperature a bit less than what feels right to you.

You will discover, while washing her two hundred and thirty-five neck folds, all the missing food that was unaccounted for during her last few feedings. At this age a baby's neck is the closest thing she has to having a pocket.

Exposing her neck for washing can pose a problem, for as you lean her backward, she will pull her chin toward her chest to stay vertical. To counter this natural reaction, I maneuver baby so her tummy is down. Now her natural reaction is to raise her head back. "Neck ready for washing, commander."

Washing baby's hair can be tricky, as you want to avoid getting any soap in her eyes or ears. I would fold each ear over against her head as I washed that side of her hair. Often I would put a folded washcloth over her eyes during the final phase of hair rinsing as well.

For some reason, all mothers and their friends smell a baby's hair first. If the hair is clean then the baby must be clean. So make sure the baby's hair is clean even if you don't have time to wash anything else.

As often as not, if it is near her bedtime, she will fall asleep during the final rinsing or the final few minutes when you place her on your shoulder before ending the shower, a quiet time for both. Here is a special moment where water conservation takes a back seat.

On occasion, following her shower and nighttime preparations, I would lay on the couch in front of the fire with her resting on her tummy on my chest. Usually she would fall asleep within five minutes, especially if I sang very quietly to her.

Now that my youngest is in her twenties, I can admit to a little white lie I was accustomed to telling my wife (I'll be forgiven after she reads this). While the two partners in crime lazed contentedly in front of the fire, MFW would gingerly approach and whisper, "Is she asleep yet?"

"No. Almost."

Actually she had been asleep for half an hour but who would want to surrender this state of bliss.

*I have but one request from God: "Please God,
when it comes to my daughters, I beg You:*
No more learning experiences!!"

6

KIDDIE MANUALS

I checked all the kiddie manuals I could locate and even read the fine print on the baby warrantees accompanying our daughters but nowhere could I find reference to a serious design flaw that seemed so pervasive—especially when they reached two. From lengthy observations I've concluded that their high level of animation and over-activity had to be a result of their being preloaded with 12-volt batteries where 6-volt batteries were specified. In addition, despite an extensive search, I've been unable to locate their on/off switch. Either it was well hidden or was omitted during assembly (nor have we ever received a product safety recall notice).

BABY WON'T STOP CRYING AT 2:00 A.M.

Why do I get the feeling all authors of baby manuals are childless bachelors who base their advice on logic? My anecdotal evidence comes from an encounter with a bachelor friend who was staying for dinner. While he made conversation, D4 began to cry seemingly without cause. Our guest, convinced D4 was crying to spite him, asked:

"Would you *please* make your baby stop crying? I'm trying to talk."

"Oh, of course. How thoughtless of me. Baby D4, would you be so kind as to stop crying so our dinner guest can continue his discourse without interruption?"

I'll admit I didn't say this but I wish I had. Our dinner guest was never heard from again.

More experienced parents know that putting your baby in an infant seat atop the dryer with a slightly unbalanced load is an effective parental trick to help Miss Precious return to Never-never land. Unfortunately to this day, all five daughters still get very groggy every time they pass a running dryer—unforeseen consequences.

Ooo, oo, oo. Another million-dollar idea.

"Yes, madam. This button is for your extended drying cycle, and this one the temperature control. This flashing green button on the end is for the asymmetric spin control designed to help put your baby to sleep at 3:00 a.m. Also, please note that the dual seat belts atop the dryer can accommodate two babies at the same time in the event you have twins, have company, or belong to a babysitting co-op."

I've gotta contact Maytag before I publish this book to see if I can cash in on my idea.

Another effective and popular trick is to take a long drive at 3:00 a.m. with baby snugly ensconced in her car seat. The boring road's white noise, the gentle rocking motion of the car, and the comfort of her seat combine to provide a wonderfully tranquilizing effect for the baby. Driving around at that time of night/morning gives one an insight into a whole society of which one would normally never be aware: people commuting to/from split shifts, garbage collectors, entertainers/entertainees, bakers, etc. However, I estimate that somewhere from 12 to 15 percent of this late/early traffic is comprised of other fathers also attempting to lull their babies back to sleep.

Perhaps someone should form a "Can't get the kid to sleep" carpool club. They could have a hotline on the Internet and, using vehicles with multiple car seats, save considerable time, fuel, and sleep. Wow, another million-dollar idea! Kidwontsleep.com. I can see it now. Two to three hundred father-infant-occupied cars roaming the highways all night being replaced by forty to fifty specially marked pink "Kidwontsleep.com" vans.

Little ones seldom fail to fall asleep on these forays but somehow always awaken within a block of returning home—totally refreshed—unlike their fathers.

We all develop goals for our daughters. Only the
disillusioned believe they will actually end up
anywhere near these goals.
"Do you believe in miracles?"
"Of course. All five of my daughters made it to
twenty-one, didn't they?"

7
ULTIMATE GOALS

We have largely realized our goals in raising our daughters, or at least they have been clever enough to convince us that we have. Our goals for D*, beyond the usual happy, healthy, and prosperous (and thinking their parents are wonderful, of course) are the big three:

1) Don't smoke.

2) Avoid drugs for the most part.

And most importantly,

3) Use adverbs correctly.

I am not so naive to think that all five have had smooth sailing in these endeavors or that they haven't experimented along the way (smoking weed could lead to something truly life-threatening like cigarettes), but as far as I know, they are mostly compliant with these three goals (coffee, red wine, and chocolate are not drugs, they are health foods).

With each of our daughters we stressed correct adverb usage from a very young age. We felt that, as they wend their way through life, they could often avoid negatively biases by just employing proper English. If one reads a printed note with numerous spelling errors, it is natural for the reader to get caught up on the errors and lose focus on the message content. In the same vein, blatant adverb abuse can undermine the impact of an otherwise brilliant dialogue.

A fourth goal is a fantasy that I'm including for parents who prefer to delude themselves. This fantasy is not unlike thinking you are bound to win the lotto even when buying one ticket a year. (The truly disillusioned are those who expect to win without buying even one ticket.)

I tried to indoctrinate each D that daughters are obligated, by duty if not by law, to remit money home to their clearly deserving parents. I figured they could start out at $100 a month at twenty-two (for practice) and gradually increase their remittance to $1,000 a month by the time they reach forty. I spent a great deal of effort to firmly implant this seed of filial responsibility into their little brains, but I have found my Ds have a genetic defect that has interfered with their ability to absorb this lesson.

MFW and I (and numerous other parents) are awaiting a scientific breakthrough that will allow us to begin corrective gene therapy as we are counting on the much-anticipated cash flow to fund our planned acquisitions, future travel plans, and expansions on our fine-dining experiences.

In the meantime, our attempt to instill guilt conditioning has failed to trigger significant generosity toward their wonderful parents (I told MFW we should never have encouraged them to think for themselves—it interferes with proper guilt conditioning).

Parents with whom I have discussed this topic love the concept. The consensus however, is to first "just get them off the payroll by forty."

So far my only token success has been D5s sending me a single dollar shortly following her twenty-second birthday, emphasizing that her generous gesture (or did she say jester?) assured her "favorite daughter" status.

If babies weren't cute, the human race
would perish.

8

TOE SANDWICH

"Waaa. Waaa. Waaaaaaaah!"

It's 2:45 a.m. Meeting at 8 a.m. Got to sleep at 1:00 a.m. Upset stomach. Headache. Somehow, this seems normal. Will I survive the night, much less the week?

I would love to look in the kiddie manual for advice on how to calm a three-year-old who is clearly in serious meltdown, confirmed by the fact I've spent the previous forty-five minutes singing to her, rocking her, carrying her around (killing my back), reasoning with her, and inquiring as to what might be the problem, all to no avail.

"Waaa. Waaa. Waaaaaaaah!"

My instincts tell me I should inquire, "Little daughter. You seem to be having some sort of difficulty here and appear to be in great distress. If you would care to describe to me, in detail, the specific symptoms that are causing you such severe discomfort, I'm sure we can address your problem or at least mitigate the source of your malaise."

"Waaa. Waaa. Waaaaaaaah."

I am confident that even half of all fathers are aware that the logical approach always proves futile in situations like this. You can see in the tot's eyes, "Don't bother me with dumb questions. Just fix it! Fix it now!" However, virtually 100 percent of all baby books and most moderately experienced mothers (those with between three and ten kids) would recommend the long list of actions I've already pursued. It takes raising somewhere between twenty and twenty-five children to understand what is actually going on here and what would be the most suitable action to take. Now since she was only daughter number four at that time, I was woefully ill prepared for my task at hand.

"Waaa! Waaa! Waaaaaaaah!"

Parents know there are at least three different types of cries. Those that are beyond the daughter's control and reflect true distress (I'm wet, I'm hungry, I'm tired, I'm sick, I'm cold), those meant to manipulate (hold me, don't leave me, entertain me, gimme my toy, add to my 401k), and those that fall in the "who knows?" category. The first type is often handled successfully by a straightforward investigation to see if a simple remedy is suitable (change diaper, feed, add blanket, etc.). The second type is often addressed successfully by singing to them, giving them a hug, putting them to bed, and rubbing their back or gently patting their head (reassurance). The third "who knows?" type is everything left over.

I know for a fact that nuclear reactor engineers borrowed the term "core meltdown" from the description of crying three-year-olds at 2:45 a.m. and not the other way around. Examination of the facts makes this conclusion obvious since crises involving little ones have been around thousands of years longer than nuclear reactors.

"Waaa! Waaa! Waaaaaaaah!"

She's past the age where old standards such as the "put the kid on the dryer" trick or the "time for a long car ride" trick are useful and too young for the "OK, you can have the car tomorrow night" concession or the equally effective "you can keep those new jeans." It's that mystical 'tween-age problem. We are breaking new ground here. So it's time to be creative—not an easy task at 2:45 a.m. Not an easy task when the subject is three years old.

LET THE REMEDY BEGIN.

"I know what you need. Of course! Why didn't I think of this earlier? You need a **Toe Sandwich!**"

Although D4 continued crying, she betrayed her interest by opening one eye a smidgen and stealing a furtive glance in my direction.

"Waaa! Waaa..."

"Ah, yes. We're lucky we have some good fresh whole wheat bread. I hate toe sandwiches made from stale bread, and white bread just isn't nutritious enough."

Crying, though not abandoned, certainly diminishes. Curiosity is a strong motivator to little ones. Now, I knew I had her attention. On to phase two.

"Now where is that ketchup? We can't have a decent toe sandwich without ketchup, and it should be really cold. Tried one with mayo once. Didn't like it."

Still sobbing but eyes locked on my activities. I ignored her as if she were but an unimportant bystander and kept my attention focused solely on gathering the ingredients for the sandwich.

"Waa. Wa."

I picked her up and set her squarely in the middle of the kitchen counter, removed her sock, brushed off, and washed her toes and placed them carefully on a slice of whole wheat bread. I next poured ketchup all over her toes, quickly topped it all off with a second slice of bread, and moved my creation toward her surprised but gaping mouth.

"Wa."

"Now I think you will really like this, so take a big bite."

"Wa. He he. Wa. He he he. He ha ha ha he he." Hysterical laughter.

"Come on, at least take a little bite. I made it 'specially for you."

"Noo, no can eat toe sandwich."

"But it's so delicious. I'll show you how. See, I'll take the first big bite."

"Noooooooo!"

Giggling, laughter, crying, smiling.

Then I held her tightly, told her how much I loved her, and confessed that she didn't really have to eat her toe sandwich if she didn't want to—at least not this time. She smiled, feigned relief, snuggled up close and after a few minutes of rocking was asleep. I washed off the ketchup and placed her in her bed. She slept through the night.

I used the threat of making her a "toe sandwich" a few times after that. The threat alone was usually sufficient to head off a pending mild meltdown.

Since then I've searched all the baby books and have yet to see any reference to making toe sandwiches. I had hoped to find hints from other fathers such as pita bread versus sliced bread or perhaps a roll would work best because of its shape. Was ketchup really the preferred condiment or would gummy bears be a better, less messy choice?

Actually I really didn't need additional information for it turns out one toe sandwich per baby daughter is quite sufficient.

"Wife, I don't care what you say. When our daughters reach thirty-eight, they are on their own!"
"Why are you are soooo mean?"

9

ART OF BEING MEAN

I am trying to perfect the art of being mean. MFW and my five Ds will all acknowledge that as far as they are concerned, I am well on my way to reaching this goal.

MFW, D4 (seven at the time), D5 (four at the time), and their favorite husband/father had just checked out of their hotel and were heading toward their parked car following a weekend of serious cavorting in Las Vegas.

At the first intersection I suggested, "Let's take this shortcut down this alley—it'll save a good five minutes."

MFW gave my practical suggestion a good 0.03 seconds of in-depth consideration, then brushed it aside with, "Oh, no. The road in front of the casinos is much more interesting, and the girls will enjoy it so much more than heading down some old alley."

I had a strong premonition when leaving the hotel that we should not venture in front of the casinos to reach our car but should instead take the safer temptation-free shortcut.

I reiterated my suggestion that the alley should be the preferred route, especially as it was so hot and the sun so bright. However, MFW was particularly adamant about her choice of direction so I relented and let it drop.

We were over halfway to the car with no hint of a potential segue so I began to feel that my apprehensions were for naught when—bam, it happened.

MFW piped up, "Oh, I still have five quarters left. I'll just pop into Harrah's and play the slots for a minute until they're history. Won't be but a minute."

My concern about taking this more circuitous casino-tempting route had been confirmed. I felt I should try to convince MFW that her stopping at Harrah's was not prudent when "poof!" she was no longer with us, but was there, just inside Harrah's door, happily disgorging her burdensome five quarters. If I had been thinking in shorter, less formal words (like, "Hey, babe, cool it"), I might have been able to act quickly enough to thwart her foray.

Fortunately for her, but unfortunately for us, she won three dollars on her first pull. After that she kept winning frequently enough so that her small grubstake refused to dwindle.

"Daddy, I'm thirsty."

"It'll just be a minute, sweetheart. Mommy will be out soon."

I knew if I ventured into the casino to gently remind her that we had a long drive ahead, she would have responded with:

"OK, just one more minute."

Now since her "one more minute" tends to be very slippery (not unlike my response to her calling me to dinner), I figured we could easily have to wait for another twenty minutes for her to finish unless she continued to win, in which case it could mushroom up to an hour.

From D5: "Daddy, I HAVE to go to the bathroom!"

Time for Plan B.

Time to be **mean.**

"D4, come here." I conferred with D4, my favorite "Partner in Mean" and we formulated a plan.

"Daddy, is Mommy coming? I really have to go to the bathroom!"

"D5, I can almost guarantee you Mommy will be out in under thirty-eight seconds."

"OK, D4, go!"

She grinned, ran into Harrah's, scooted behind security, right up to her mother's side, gave her mother's sleeve several sharp yanks and shouted.

"Mommy! Mommy! No, Mommy! Not the rent money! You promised!"

*Chauffeuring your teenage daughter and her
friends is the next best thing to reading her diary.*

1 0

Tips

CHAUFFEURING

Chauffeur your offspring and their friends as often as you can, particularly when they are between twelve and fifteen. If she is going to a movie with her friends, don't let other parents do the driving. The information you will glean in one hour of being the fly-on-the-rearview-mirror chauffeur will exceed months of intense direct interrogation. Drive, keep quiet, and turn the "attention control" on your ears up to max. Within ten minutes they will talk about everything as if you didn't exist. Remember, as far as they are concerned, most of the time parents don't exist anyway, so for once in your life you can use this usually annoying trait to your advantage. Don't say a word (not easy—takes a great deal of restraint—ommmm) for if you break their fantasy of your being invisible with a touch of reality, i.e., "Are any of you girls hungry?" or "How's your mother?" (a double no-no), you will have to bide your time an additional ten to fifteen minutes before they comfortably settle back into "The Zone."

If, in response to something you overhear you interject, "She kissed who?" you can forget having access to the intimate details of their conversations for at least a two-month probation period. You will have totally shut down your access to this valuable source of inside information. It would be akin to a secret wiretapper breaking into a private phone call with, "Could you repeat that, please? I didn't get the last couple of words."

Your job: provide the water bottles, carry the tools or any spare parts that may be needed for their equipment, peel the oranges, help officiate, be the stat recorder, help her friends at sporting events when their parents can't make it, talk to other parents, watch the practices, buy the school project supplies, chaperone the dances, host the cast parties, be the parent advisor for their small-group projects, run their short errands and stay out of the way. Provide the sleepover headquarters, the after-school community gathering place and keep the treat refrigerator fully stocked (thirty percent of which will certainly end up being devoted to this purpose).

Avoid the large planning organizations. These involve a great deal of time and little insight into your young'ns' day-to-day lives. Don't feel guilty because you are not on certain school committees. Between chauffeuring and chaperoning, you are doing more than your share. As a former Stanford dean and friend of MFW advised, "**Volunteer where the kids are.**" The power behind the power comes from being invisible.

TRAVEL

Stretch the minds of these experience sponges with travel when they are ready. Taking kids on expensive trips when they are too young isn't cost effective. I asked a friend's seven-year-old how he liked his trip to Rome with his parents. All he remembered was playing Ping-Pong at their famous and rather overpriced hotel.

D1 was three when we returned from Kwajalein in the Marshall Islands, about twenty-three hundred miles west of Hawaii, back to Boston so I could continue my schooling. Two years later, while preparing to head back for a second tour on Kwaj, one of D1's friends asked her where Kwajalein was. Pointing to the horizon she answered, "You go over that hill— over there to Hawaii and turn left." Close enough.

Ironically travel often provides an opportunity for family togetherness that would normally be thought of as a home activity – particularly the "cabin in the mountains" type of vacation. The unscheduled intervals during travel can be filled with doing a jigsaw puzzle together or playing board games. Such doings are usually usurped at home by the backlog of home maintenance demands. These family activities during travel often make the biggest impressions on the little ones for it is during this time they finally have your full attention.

COPE

After a particularly difficult day trying to cope with a teenage daughter, MFW and I would go to bed and remind each other, "OK, it's you and me." Or, "Remember, only 945 more days until she is out on her own." Of course, eighteen months later we both become depressed at the mere thought of her leaving our abode for college because we knew we would miss her so much—she had become so wonderful!

I've always had to keep reminding myself that the Ds are "works in progress" and that they will change on short notice. We must not become overly concerned about any single snapshot in time. MFW and I try to look at them as "objects of interest" rather than their being our total second-to-second responsibility, which works just fine as long as they are not threatened or in danger. Then, watch out.

Of course, after a particularly bad day we would occasionally turn to each other and ask, "So tell me again. Why did we have children?" Or, "My daughters? I thought they were your daughters!" Or again, "What do you mean you turned down eight camels for our seventeen-year-old daughter? The least you could have done was to ask me first."

Since all our daughters are alive and well today, the reader can infer that any drastic option that might have been on the table at one time or another was never actually implemented.

A prime example, which every parent firmly understands, is the first time they drop D* off at her new nursery school or at the babysitter's. The daughter unit will make a huge scene, employing expert panic-pleading for you not to leave her. Her show will, of course, be accompanied by a torrent of tears gushing down her distorted grief-torn face. This image of her, burned deep into your retinas, will haunt you the rest of the day at work and you will continually reprimand yourself for being such an incredibly bad parent. "How could I have done this to my fragile, sensitive daughter?" Guilt, guilt, guilt. Of course the daughter unit will have forgotten even who you are thirty seconds after you've left and will immediately begin having a wonderful time playing—the little heart-string trouncer. Did I mention guilt?

Daughter, age sixteen, would not come to dinner so I went to investigate. I found her in a fetal posture in the corner of the closet crying. "I have no friends. I have no life." My natural nurturing instincts made me want to rush to her aid and fight off the evil social dragons of teenage cliquedom that were tormenting my perfect daughter. Then I realized that her phone, which she ignored, wouldn't stop ringing. If she had no friends, then who was responsible for this incessant stream of calls—telemarketers? Later I learned that she had overheard one classmate, whom she didn't even like (in fact, no one liked), say what could possibly have been interpreted as a disparaging remark about her. Did I mention before how I didn't, don't, and never will understand teenage girls?

A few hours later life went on as if nothing had ever happened—at least for her. To her it is long lost and forgotten yet I still remember it well enough to put it in print ten years later.

Advice: don't try to keep up, especially with their micro events, as you will find yourself on the wrong planet. It's often best if we just don't know.

If eye rolling (at my jokes) were an Olympic sport,
my daughters would all be medal contenders.

1 1

EXPERT ADVICE —
NOT

The experts, feeding their brand of advice to parents, are well meaning, highly educated with strong credentials, certainly confident, and dispense a lot of good information. During all of their research however, many of them could use more than a few minutes of "quality time" with a blood-related teenager. Here are a few of my favorite pieces of "advice."

TV

"Try to limit your children's TV to ten hours a week and encourage them to spend more time reading."

My reaction, "You've gotta be kidding!" Even when D4 was eight, she was usually too busy reading to watch TV. Getting her to watch a program with us for even an hour a week was the best we could hope for.

When for some minor home-rule infraction, we needed to discipline D4, nothing seemed to work. If we sent her to her room she went willingly and seemed content to be by herself. We couldn't restrict her viewing TV because she had no interest in watching it in the first place. Nothing worked.

Finally, we hit on the one thing she really cared about—reading.

"If you don't [fill in the blank], we won't let you read for an hour."

This was a threat she took seriously, and the first few times we restricted her access to books were moderately effective. After a few weeks of employing this new form of discipline however, she ceased protesting and took her punishment in stride. Her ready acquiescence of this discipline seemed suspect at the time, but we gave it no further thought. A few months later we discovered why she complied so readily with our new approach. This creative young lady had a secret stash. There were books hidden all throughout the house.

We found her partially read books under towels in the bathroom, at the bottom of her sock drawer, atop the cabinet in the spare room, and under the sink in the guest bathroom. One more example of how seriously under-equipped parents are in their attempts to keep up with a daughter.

COMMUNICATION

"Sit down with your child several times a week and have informative and confidential chats with them. Let them know you can discuss anything at length with them without their feeling ill at ease."

Sounds good.

When D5 was fifteen, I was self-employed and would usually be working in our home office about the time she returned from school. Coming into the house she would stride past my desk, at which time I'd take the opportunity to engage her in some form of discourse. I always inquired as to how her day went or whether anything new happened in school. As my imperfect memory recalls, our typical routine went something like this:

Monday: "Hello, D5, how was school today?"

"Fine."

Tuesday: "Oh, I see you are limping less today. Is your foot better?"

"It's fine."

Wednesday. "How did swim practice go?"

"Fine."

Thursday: "How did blah blah blah?"

"Fine."

Friday: "Blah blah blah...?"

"Fine."

Next week: Monday... Thursday, same.

Friday I was out on an errand when she came home and didn't get back until an hour after her arrival.

I entered the kitchen to find her standing there waiting for me. With her hands defiantly set on her hips, legs planted firmly on the floor, and a stern penetrating stare pinning me to the wall, she demanded, **"Where were you?"**

I wanted to say, "Oh, I'm so sorry we missed our daily incredibly in-depth, meaningful conversation today. Please forgive me!" But I thought any humor in my sarcastic answer would be lost so I played it straight—well, almost. My actual response went something like, "Oh, I am so sorry. I was late because I was trying to purchase a very expensive present for you."

Two communicating extremes can be observed within minutes. Put three teenage girls online at the same time and the entire Internet will be brought to its knees throughout the country due to serious data overload. In contrast, ask your teenage daughter anything about her life and you will discover that the aggregate information in her responses, even in an hour's time, could easily be written on the back of a credit card receipt.

Proper English

"Try to use proper English and grammar around your children to improve their general communication skills."

I thought I had this one under control. The primary infractions in our home were adverbs so I cleverly (or so I thought) instigated a system of fines. Nothing like a few monetary incentives to get everyone's attention. A fine of ten cents was to be levied against any member of the family making an adverb error, payable to the adverb error detector. I cleared a little over $2.10 that first week but from then on it was all downhill. The second week I netted $1.20, the third only $0.40. Ever since the fourth week I have been paying out a couple bucks a week more than I have been taking in. Once D4 and D5 realized that this system of fines was now working to their advantage, they voted to raise the fines to $0.25. I protested their lack of fairness in raising the fines unilaterally (MFW took their side) but seemed powerless to do anything about it. Be sure to add this idea to your list of unanticipated expenses in raising daughters.

An example of how the tables were turned on me by my uncompromising daughters:

(in the early days) Father, after an appropriate "Aha!"

"D4, you owe me a dime."

"No, I don't."

"You didn't use that adverb correctly."

"But that was an idiomatic expression so I don't owe you anything."

"Not in this house. Fork it over."

"You are so unfair."

(six months later) D4, after an appropriate double "Aha!" "Aha!" (D4 is more dramatic in her "Ahas" than her favorite father is.)

"Daddy, you owe me a quarter."

"No, I don't."

"You didn't use that adverb correctly."

"But that was an idiomatic expression so I don't owe you anything."

"Not in this house. Fork it over."

"You're so unfair."

"Any more whining, and we'll raise the fine for each infraction to a dollar."

I can report with certainty, however, that they have superb adverb usage, at least around adults. I haven't caught them making an adverb error in years. I, on the other hand, still slip up occasionally and, since my daughters are ruthless, they won't let me out of the game. They have come to rely on the "adverb game" as a dependable source of revenue.

I did make it clear to them from the beginning that they could talk in any way they wanted with their friends as long as they knew how to speak to adults. Basically I told them they needed to be bilingual, i.e., fluent in both teen-speak and adult-speak.

Don't even try to intimidate me. Compared to the
women in my life, you are basically a non-event.

1 2

DAUGHTER

(First syllable often spelled: Duh)

Definition: A female offspring of a mother and father whose usual DNA mix is statistically derived 50 percent from the father and 50 percent from the mother. Miracles have been known to occur wherein the male DNA half appears to have been derived from some unknown source (although milkmen, neighbors, and UPS men are suspect), from virgin births (often associated with religions or convenient face-saving fabrications), or from causes such as getting pregnant from a toilet seat or a swimming pool. Although this last postulation is highly improbable, one never knows what physiological effects occur in a pool filled with twenty teenaged boys surrounded by a few well-proportioned bikini-clad teenage girls.

DERIVATION SOURCE

Duh, first syllable, is believed to have evolved from an eighth-century Western-American-Indian noun, "dada" (or "duhduh"), meaning clueless or inept and was first coined by infant girls to describe their instinctual feelings about the male gender and their possible value to society other than hunting. It may also be used as an adverb or adjective to describe certain situations or individuals.

Duh:

The root word "duh" has recently enjoyed a resurgence of popularity during the last twenty years by young women who find it quite succinct in describing their parents' near total lack of understanding (particularly the fathers) of the young person's modern world. They also apply this word to boys of their own age when assessing their three- to seven-year lag in social skill development. Young boys often try to apply "duh" but are really only emulating girls and don't fully comprehend either its use or in-depth meanings.

Some scholars claim that the extension of "duh" to "duh-tear" (pronounced daughter) occurred as a result of the large quantity of tears shed in frustration by fathers trying to understand their female offsprings, but this theory has not enjoyed wide acceptance.

"Duh" has been studied extensively by numerous high-profile linguists for years who, to date, have made only partial progress in decoding its incredibly large expanse of meanings due to its wide range of complex tonal qualities.

This type of tonal complexity can be illustrated by an often-cited example. The Chinese word "ma" can have four separate meanings depending on the tonality used in its pronunciation. Mother, open flat tone; numb, rising tone; horse, down-up tone; and scold, falling tone. (I'm not sure how you would say, "Mother scolds the numb horse.")

As of this writing, linguists have been able to identify, with certainty, a minimum of seventeen distinct tonal varieties in a teenage daughter's application of "duh" to adults (especially her father), and four more when applying it to teenage boys (young girls know young boys are so underdeveloped that four tones pretty well covers it all). There are hints that as many as forty-one additional tones may exist, which, if true, would make "duh" the highest tonal variant word yet identified across all world languages. The problem stems from the fact that applications of variation forms of "duh" are not unlike certain viruses that mutate almost as rapidly as they can be identified.

After living with five daughters, the easiest part in becoming a devout monk would be the oath of silence.

1 3

PANTHER TRACKS: DAD/DAUGHTER BANTER

After a protracted discussion with D4, I went totally against her wishes and volunteered to chaperone her seventh/ eighth-grade middle school dances. Every middle schooler begrudgingly accepts the fact that: no chaperones, no dances. At the same time they add: "But not my parents!" While chaperoning her first dance, I mentioned to the principal how much fun it was witnessing these boy-girl pre-puberty rituals. She commented she wished more parents felt this way as they were having difficulty recruiting chaperones for these dances— especially fathers. After witnessing my positive take on my whole experience, she asked if I would write an article for their local PTA publication, The Panther Tracks, in hopes it might encourage other fathers to also volunteer.

I submitted my article two days later. The publication staff (parent volunteers) initially objected, citing the mission of the publication was solely to inform parents and teachers of schedules and school issues. The principal read my contribution aloud at the planning meeting. They loved it—no dissenters.

My daughter, D4, discovered my intention and, horrified that I would put her in a bad light, declared that she would write the rebuttal. "No way!" said the publication staff. "We certainly don't want students writing for our publication." Then they read her contribution. "My goodness—the daughter writes better than the father. In it goes."

We contributed dueling articles in eight issues over the next two years. We were told that these articles generated the only requests for extra copies in the history of the publication.

We never signed our articles with our real names. I often signed I.P., for Involved Parent, and D4 signed MISK, for MIddle School Kid. Several of these article/rebuttals are included in this book.

"HOW CAN I POSSIBLY GROW UP NORMAL IN A FAMILY LIKE THIS?"

*"You can't. Now get down off your chair, sit down,
and finish your dinner."
"Oh. OK."
D4's one and only effort to be normal - failed.*

1 4

Panther Tracks I

YIKES! DAD'S CHAPERONING

JUST BORING PARENTS STUFF (FROM THE FATHER UNIT)

There are certain recent social activities about which I wish to share my interpretation and how they involve adult members of the community. My topic is chaperoning middle school dances.

I feel a bit like the first discoverers at Sutter's Mill in 1848. Each one would have been far better off if they could have kept their newfound discovery a secret for as long as possible instead of blabbing about it. I truly enjoy chaperoning these dances and find that the lack of interest from other fathers has thus far worked to my advantage. Forgive me for not revealing my name but I have a daughter who, although acknowledging the need for parental presence, is not pleased that I am an active member of this chaperoning population.

Before my first foray into this new role as chaperone to last year's final dance (where sixth graders were included), I sat down with my daughter to discuss "the rules." She immediately took over the conversation.

"Dad, there are three rules:

"One. You are not to tell anyone that you're my father. Two. You are not to look in my direction at any time. And, three. You are not to tell any jokes."

She then promptly rose, turned, and marched out of the room. Well, I was certainly glad we had had this little chat to straighten things out.

Middle school is an awful time for students. Middle school is a wonderful time for students. Take your pick or better yet pick both. Uncertainty reigns. Who likes whom? How to be cool but not standoffish? What's important? Who to ask questions of when you're convinced you're supposed to know these things?

I discovered that inviting half a dozen of my daughter's friends over for pizza an hour before the dance and then becoming invisible was an excellent way for them to start the evening. Anticipation builds excitement, and an hour among friends builds confidence and camaraderie. I would then bus the whole group to the dance and let them melt into the chaos.

I assumed my first post and tried not to notice my offspring. There seem to be several phases to these events, and I'm not sure I can do their descriptions justice. Phase one involves meeting friends with a great deal of accompanying commotion. This is followed by an assessment of the music quality and an exploration of the facilities to learn the lay of the land. More friends are spotted and acknowledged. Focus on friends and other safe activities such as evaluating each other's hair, fingernail polish and wardrobe and sharing their knowledge of the latest dance steps continues for an hour or so with a gradual coalescing in the dance area. A few "items" may break the ice by dancing first, and gradually, midway through the dance, "it" begins.

The pace slackens, the lights dim, some finding of each other occurs, albeit at a distance. He asks himself if he should ask her to dance; he does. She makes an excuse to say no. He wonders if he did the right thing. She hopes he'll ask again. And so on.

The cubs are leaving their den for the first time. The flowers, though not ready to bloom, are getting ready to bud. Who cannot feel spring in the air, the rebirth, the remembering? Here, they are trying to take control but not sure what or how to control. My respect and admiration for them increase a great deal at these dances.

I watch four students dance in a circle with arms joined around the shoulders; then it's six, then ten. A wallflower walks by, is pulled into the dance, and for a short time, she belongs. There is a surprising lack of negativity and far more innocence than I expected. Twenty form a dance troop and go through their routine. A couple is slow dancing; then a third joins by placing his hands on one of the dancer's shoulders from behind. Then a fourth behind him and then more until up to a dozen will be in a line behind each other dancing with a single partner. These experiences are all new to me, not part of my generation. These kids, while not perfect, may have far to go but they are a good group. I get the feeling that our presence is both tolerated and appreciated. Our role is to be present and invisible at the same time. An over-exuberance is often calmed merely by an adult walking by. The potential problems in the boys' bathrooms disappear after the first half hour; after that they're empty, as none of the boys wants to miss anything.

The last ten minutes hasten courage, or perhaps it's just that a critical mass has finally reached the comfort level. Then it is over. All data have been collected for detailed analysis over the next few days. The ride home should be as long as possible so preliminary assessments can be made. I always take the participant who lives the furthermost away home first so the discussions can continue uninterrupted. The parent-driver is well-advised to feign listening to the radio during this time to maintain the impression that he is not involved.

I'm really positive on these dances and encourage more parents to witness these rites of passage. You will gain some insight into this remarkable period in your child's life. Be warned, in a time far too short, poof, they will be gone.

—I.P. (Involved Parent)

Daughter's Rebuttal

To: Readers, Parents, and most of all, my Dad.

After discovering that my father submitted an article to Panther Tracks without my knowledge, I decided I need to put things in the correct light. But first I must have a word with my father. Dad, how **dare** you write an article and send it in without my permission!

To begin with, I am fully aware that without chaperones, we cannot have dances; therefore, I encourage all parents to chaperone — except mine. Parents, I would like to point out that there are four rules instead of three that parents should follow, and I am pretty sure that most of your kids will agree:

Rule Number 1) You are not to let anyone know whose mother or father you are.

Rule Number 2) You are not to look or even glance at your son or daughter, or even in his or her direction.

Rule Number 3) (and the most important one in my opinion). Do not tell ANY jokes!! This one is a must. And finally,

Rule Number 4) Do not speak until you are spoken to. Chaperones are to be barely seen and not heard.

You must understand, parents, that these four rules are for your own good as well as your child's. I must admit that even though I don't like you chaperoning, Dad, you do follow the rules better than Mom, and I do like the pizza and the ride home with my friends, so I have come to a compromise. When the next dance comes, why don't you chaperone the tennis courts?

—signed, "Distressed"

Daughter lecturing father on chaperoning rules:

1) Do not tell anyone whose father you are.
2) Do not look or even glance in my direction.
3) This is a must! Do not tell any jokes!
4) Do not speak until you are spoken to. Chaperones are to be barely seen and not heard.

When I was young, all the dogs in the cartoons were male and all the cats, female. I finally realized it was because dogs were trainable and cats were not.

1 5

WARNING

After an onsite inspection by the EMPA (Environmental Male Protection Agency), I have been provided with a sign shown on the following page to identify the potential perils that may befall any male over twelve, should he inadvertently stray into our compound. On advice of my lawyer, I display this sign prominently over the portico of our kitchen. More than one male, unaware of the intensity of our estrogen-laden environment, has expressed gratitude for my thoughtfulness in keeping him apprised.

Other overconfident machismo males who have not heeded this warning have been found crouching in a corner, shaking and muttering to themselves.

Warning

The government has determined that this facility contains an abnormally high level of the chemical estrogen known to induce severe male disorientation. Common symptoms may include inability to get a word in, a sense that no one is listening, a feeling that everyone thinks it's all his fault, and an unexpectedly heavy drain on his financial resources.

A daughter who never loses to her father in a Sudoku challenge shows disrespect, which could seriously endanger her allowance.

MAY I HELP YOU?

Ring...Ring...Ring...

"Hello. XZY Corporation. This is Anna. How may I help you?"

I pause on purpose.

"Hello. XZY Corporation. This is Anna. How may I help you?"

"I'm sorry, my phone keeps cutting out on me. Could you repeat that please?"

"Certainly. This is XZY Corporation, and this is Anna speaking. May I help you?"

"No, thank you. I don't need any help right now but it's so nice of you to ask. In fact this is the first time a female has asked if she could help me since I called ABC Corporation a month ago. And I just want to say—" Click.

Ring...Ring...Ring...

"Hello. TUV Corporation. This is Brenda. Do you need assistance?"

"I don't think so but my wife claims I've needed help for years and—" Click.

Ring...Ring...Ring...

"Hello. PQR Corporation. This is Louise. How may I help you?"

"My daughter's tuition is due in a week so anything you could spare would be most appreciated."

Click.

Ring...Ring...Ring...

"Hello. MNO Corporation. This is Helga. How may I direct your call?"

"Could you please direct my call to my daughters? Maybe they would listen to you if you asked them to call me because—"

Click.

Ring...Ring...Ring...

"Hello. JKL Corporation. This is Kathy. May I help you?"

"No, thanks. With five daughters I'm told I'm beyond help. But thanks anyway.

Contrary to my daughters' insistence, waking a teenage daughter before noon on a Saturday, although certainly unappreciated, does not constitute child abuse.

17

THEY DID EARN MONEY

Is it possible that my whole take on this "where has all the money gone?" *syndrome* (to be sung to the tune of *Where Have All the Flowers Gone*) is just paranoia on my part? I distinctly remember several of my daughters working hard to achieve their goals.

D3 flew in from her home in Colorado to join us for a few weeks in Northern California when she was thirteen. Both MFW and I were only a few years out of graduate school and the income needed to supply child support for three daughters plus a newly acquired mortgage meant money was pretty scarce.

On her third day, she brought up a subject that clearly had been on her mind for months.

"Daddy, you won't let me have a horse."

"No, you can have a horse."

Two days later.

"Daddy, you won't let me have a horse."

"No, you can have a horse."

Over the next few days.

Repeat, repeat, repeat.

Finally, on the day she was to return,

"Daddy, you won't *buy* me a horse."

"I'm afraid you're right. We can't afford to buy you a horse so the best we can do at this time is to encourage you to figure out how to buy a horse on your own."

She returned to Boulder determined to make it happen. She bought a horse a few weeks later for fifty dollars and traded working at a local ranch for its board. Disaster. She ended up trading the bad-news horse for a pair of roller skates within the month.

She applied for a job as a hostess at a nearby restaurant in hopes of earning her way to securing a decent horse. During the interview when asked, "Are you sixteen?" She responded, "No. But my birthday is October 18th."

"That's only a few weeks away. I guess we can start you a few weeks early without getting into too much trouble. How about three days a week from 4:00 p.m. to 8:00 p.m. starting Monday?"

"Great."

She got her job, bought and trained her horse, Moonshadow, won her share of ribbons showing and racing barrels, and became an accomplished and happy cowgirl.

It wasn't until two years later that her employer was shocked to discover they had actually hired a thirteen year old. She had used her 5'9" height to push the envelope by two years.

While carding at the door of a catering job for the same restaurant, she admitted a seventeen-year-old friend into a

"You Gotta be Eighteen" event (before the beer drinking age was raised to twenty-one).

The big boss strolled over and asked, "Are you sure that kid's eighteen?"

"I'm as sure that he's eighteen as I am eighteen."

"Oh. OK then."

D3 was fifteen at the time.

During summer break from college, she signed on as the head wrangler at a dude ranch in the mountains near Estes Park—her horse pursuits paid off after all. She did complain that the young cowboys working for her kept getting hurt and had to be replaced.

"You know. They just don't make them like they used to."

When D2 and D3 visited me in Boulder (while I was working on my Ph.D.) during their summer vacations, they would often work with me at Nancy's Restaurant on Sundays where I washed dishes mostly for fun and to be a part of "the family" of Nancy's crew. I agreed with Nancy to work for food credits but, with a single exception while wooing MFG (later to become MFW), I never got around to collecting on this arrangement.

At six and eight, D3 and D2 would do the topping and prepping for the breakfast omelets, sort the tableware, and put away the dishes. Nancy would pay them in cash under the entry "tomatoes." So my little tomatoes would earn a few dollars on each visit while having fun helping in the kitchen.

One Sunday, I happened to enter the kitchen at the same time as Nancy. The only workers in the kitchen as we entered were Kim, her fourteen-year-old apprentice cook, Nancy's five-year-old son doing the prepping, and D2, my eight-year-old daughter, doing the topping—average age, nine.

I couldn't resist turning to Nancy and asking, "So tell me, Nancy. Just how are you able to keep your kitchen labor costs so low?"

To cut the catering costs at her own wedding, D1, with D2's help, worked from 2:00 a.m. to 7:00 a.m. on her wedding day preparing all the dishes that would be needed for the big event. The restaurant where she worked volunteered the ingredients; all she had to do was take care of the preparations. Since we provided her with a lump sum for her wedding expenses—this meant money saved for other things.

All five Ds worked when they could to help with their expenses. D5 became her own paint contractor in San Diego during her junior year summer vacation. She made cold calls, bid her own jobs, hired and trained her painters, and arranged for materials, scheduling, and transportation to complete the jobs. The most difficult aspect of this work was that twice she had to fire friends. They just couldn't produce to the standards she needed from them to make a go of it.

She later discovered that by working for her school's catering she could get fed in addition to being paid. Plus the catering delivery golf carts became a great "let me drop you off/pick you up at your class" benefit shared by the student caterers.

For ten years, starting at thirteen, D4 plied us at every opportunity with her philosophy that young women should not be allowed to model.

"It's an exploitation of women. It makes them objects instead of real people with real feelings. They are being used to further the industrial..."

You get the drift. She was an adamant socialist-feminist not shy about sharing her ideas and ideology with her clearly clueless parents, especially during dinner time.

I can now report that the year I began this book, she earned more income in one year as a model than I ever did as an overeducated engineer. So how come I was never able to be exploited as successfully as she was? Where did I go wrong?

Parent of a teenage daughter to spouse: "Could you explain to me one more time? Why was it we had children?"

1 8

IT'S YOU AND ME

A close friend and MFW were taking a well-deserved popcorn/gin & tonic break one late summer afternoon when the oft-visited topic of paying our teenage daughters' looming college education expenses surfaced yet again.

"Have you seen the new tuitions at some of these public colleges? And I'd hate to think what a private school would run, plus room and board, plus..."

"Don't forget pocket money, books, health insurance, travel..."

"It's not that far away, so we'd better figure out some way to finance this monster."

"Problem is we're stuck in that middle income group—too poor to afford to pay for their college and too rich to get any help."

"Maybe scholarship, work study, extortion, loans, marry rich, summer job, rob a bank, junior college..."

Tuesday: friend shows up.

"Don't worry. It's not a problem. If I have to go through one more day like this, with my daughter's back talk, I'll make sure she never makes it to her fourteenth birthday anyway!"

What a surprise. Sometimes little Miss Perfect seems 180 degrees out of character. For those parents who have exhausted all patience, remedies, techniques, last resorts and last-last resorts, I have bad news. You will be disappointed to learn that it's euthanasia and not youth-anasia that some states are trying to legalize. My research has thus far shown that youth-anasia is still illegal in at least forty-three if not all fifty states (plus the District of Columbia and Puerto Rico).

Granted, if a jury were comprised of only mothers of thirteen- and fourteen-year-old girls, there is a good chance the verdict would be either "almost justified homicide" or "non-premeditated youth-anasia" (i.e., a crime of extreme passion involving a mother and teenage daughter also known as "fifth-degree murder" with a mandatory two-week suspended sentence).

I did overhear one mother of a thirteen-year-old daughter whisper secretly to another in a waiting room with that look on her face, "Are you sure it's too late to get an abortion? I thought the age limit was fifteen." Sympathetic companion responded, "Actually, I think retroactive abortions are not allowed in any event."

In 2003, economists Gordon Dahl (University of Rochester) and Enrico Moretti (UCLA) came up with the findings that parents with only girls are more likely to get divorced than families with only boys, and this divorce rate gap increases as the number of daughters/sons in the family increases.

To me and any other father of daughters, this conclusion is one of those no-brainers. "I could have told you that and saved all that research money. It could have been better spent for say, a 'multi-daughtered' father recovery program.'"

I have to be fair and mention that this statistic includes Asian countries where extra premiums are placed on having sons. Come to think of it, Henry the VIII had the same attitude but relied on an alternate and more permanent solution than divorce.

Teaser question heard on TV as part of an advertisement to interest viewers in attending a colloquium on marriage relations: "What is the major source of stress leading to divorce?" As part of the ad they volunteered that the answer is neither a partner having an affair nor money. They claimed it was children—particularly young children. They further claimed that a marriage involving teenaged stepdaughters had the greatest chance of ending in a divorce—close to 100 percent.

My heart really goes out to the truly underprivileged class—the single mother (or, less often, single father if they retain custody), particularly when they reach that state because of a partner's bailing out due to the stress of raising children. If it is too stressful for a couple to handle, think what it's like for a single mother or single father (my situation for a while with my first three daughters) to carry the burden alone.

So how do couples survive the strain? Love with a tacit understanding that the burden must be shared.

"OK. Now remember. In the long run, it's *YOU and ME.*"

Then, just when Planned Parenthood contacts you requesting permission to use your specific family as their prime example of why birth control can sometimes be a good idea, POW. The heavens open, choirs sing, rainbows and butterflies are everywhere, and Miss Pain-in-the-wicky-wicky morphs into Miss Incredible-wonderful-sweet-joy. The tunnel has been traversed. Your daughter is wonderful. Joy, joy, joy!

"Hello, Mom. I'm calling you just to tell I love you and I really do appreciate all you've done for me."

"Who is this? What have you done with my daughter? You put her on this minute!"

After this seemingly spontaneous transformation, the only problem is the fear that someday she will leave. Suddenly each young suitor is no longer considered a potential savior who may someday take her off your hands, but a lustful predator who clearly isn't anywhere good enough for her, this saint of yours, your most precious daughter.

Pavlovian response to "Daddy, can I ..." is a
father's reaching for his wallet.

19

DAYDREAMS

I spend a lot of time waiting patiently for my chance to speak during multi-daughter/wife conversation competitions. Although this might be a bit of a shock to them, I am not always completely engrossed in their topics, especially when they are laced with special female code words—words I wouldn't be able to comprehend even if they were explained, re-explained and re-re-explained to me. At times like this, my mind begins to wander, and I either begin to work silently on calculations that currently impact our living standards or plunge full-fledged into daydreams.

Talk, talk, talk. Drone, drone, drone.

"May I see your driver's license, please?"

"Certainly officer. But what's the matter? I know I'm not speeding since I'm parked."

"That's just the problem. You're sitting in a disabled parking space and are not displaying a disabled parking placard."

"But I was just about to leave."

"No matter. You are violating the law and occupying a space that may be needed for the convenience of someone less fortunate."

"I'm sorry, officer. Here is my license."

"Wait, what's that? What's that in your wallet?"

"Oh, that's a photo of my five daughters."

"You have five daughters?"

"Yeah, and no sons."

"Oh, I'm sooo sorry. If I had known, I wouldn't have bothered you. Is there any way I can be of assistance to you? Is one parking spot enough? Hey, lady! Put that wheelchair back in your car and move your car over! Can't you see this man needs more room! If there is any way my department can help, please, just call 911."

Drone, drone, drone. Talk, talk, talk.

They are still talking without taking breaks to breathe. I'll wait. It shouldn't be much longer.

Talk, talk, talk. Drone, drone, drone.

"Mr. Jacobson, might I have a word with you before you leave?"

"Certainly. But first I want to tell you how much I appreciate being in your stress management class. MFW was right. I should have signed up for this class years ago."

"I'm not sure how to tell you this. I just wondered if you wouldn't mind searching for some alternate class to sign up for."

"I don't understand. I thought this class was a perfect fit for me."

"Well, yes—for you perhaps. But several of my other students have confided in me that, if you remain, they will have to drop out."

"But why? I haven't offended anybody, have I?"

"Oh, no, nothing like that. Everyone likes you so that's not the issue at all. It's just, well, they find listening to your experiences with your daughters too stressful for them. They can't handle it."

Great. I'm not only flunking my stress management class but am taking everyone else down with me.

Drone, drone, drone. Talk, talk, talk.

Oh good, a break in the conversation.

"D4, D5, can I speak to you for a minute?"

"We'd love to, Dad, but we're already fifteen minutes late. We'll talk to you when we get back."

"And at what time might that be?"

"Oh, it should be sometime not long after 3:00 a.m. Bye, Daddy."

"Bye. Oh, do either of you need any money?"

"Well, $40 would help. Thanks, Dad. Yeah, bye. Love ya."

"So tell us, D5, if you could have anything
for Christmas your little heart desired,
what would it be?"
"I want to be an only child."

2 0

BABY BIRD

Conceded: Teenagers are the most difficult population subset to wake up in the morning, particularly as the employment of both dynamite and high pressure water hoses is no longer permitted as teenager wake-up tools. Waking a six- or seven-year-old daughter, no matter how nice, can also be a challenge on school day mornings. Their angelic sleeping face precludes employing the drastic techniques reserved for the more recalcitrant teens.

Ah, there is a way. A method that is gentle, fun, and even nutritious (I kid you not). It's the "Baby Bird" routine.

Time: 7:10 a.m. on a school day.

Location: Bedroom of a seven-year-old daughter who stayed up late and therefore has accumulated a two-hour sleep deficit.

Action: Father (who has accumulated a four-hour sleep deficit) enters room with three cold peeled orange boats in his left hand and one orange boat held aloft in his right hand, – executing various flying maneuvers through the air.

"Baby Bird, time for your worm. Baby Bird, here comes Daddy Bird [Mommy Bird never sounded right to me] with a nice fresh worm. Open wide."

Baby Bird makes a small movement; then opens her mouth slightly. Other than that, she seems motionless and keeps her eyes shut. Flying orange boat makes a few more sorties about the room with accompanying swishing sounds then touches Baby Bird's lips. Mouth opens more widely. Worm enters Baby Bird's beak. Mouth closes with slight squishing sound. Trace of small smile becomes evident on Baby Bird's face. Eyes remain shut in an attempt to safeguard her world of slumber.

Second worm appears in right hand of Daddy Bird.

"Baby Bird. Here comes another worm for Baby Bird. Open wide for your yummy super delicious worm."

Baby Bird opens, closes, crunches on second worm, and smiles. Pretense of being asleep is abandoned. By the fourth worm Baby Bird is awake and happy. Any animosity arising from being woken "before her time" dissolves, and she sits up, ready to take on the world.

She has been woken by the pleasant flavor of fresh, cold, juicy orange boats, which stimulate both her taste buds and her appetite. Her breakfast has begun. Voilà!

As a daughter gets a few years older the success of this early morning ritual can be prolonged by adding hot tea to her orange slices.

*A seriously sleep deprived friend and father of a
two year old confided in me, "Now I know why
they call it the terrible twos."
"No, you don't. The real reason is to lull you
into a false sense of hope by not telling you that
following the terrible twos are the terrible threes,
the terrible fours, the terrible fives, the terrible..."*

2 1

Panther Tracks II

THE BLIND MEN
HAD IT EASY

We are all familiar with the fable of the group of blind men trying to describe their first encounter with an elephant. They couldn't agree on a common description as each had examined a different portion of the elephant's anatomy. Each was correct in what he knew but, not being aware of the larger picture or the many ways of seeing the same truth, was convinced his associates were in error. Frankly, these men had it easy compared to the efforts that parents make in trying to reconcile with their middle schoolers. At least the object of the blind men's attention was both corporeal and a fixed target.

The parent-offspring relationship is purely abstract, illogical, and anything but fixed. In my ten years of experience garnered over these past ten months, I've gathered a few thoughts about a small part of this conundrum that I'm sharing here as much to solicit camaraderie and sympathy as to help other parents caught in the same quandary.

I'm convinced a major area of conflict arises purely from sensory differences. A middle schooler's metabolism is so high that she truly needs one less layer of clothing on a cool day than her parents do. If physically active (e.g., basketball, soccer, dance) or generally excited (an important phone call), this difference increases another level or two. Our insistence that our D add a sweater on her way out the door is not received gracefully by an already overheated adolescent. Until I see a headline reading, "Seventh grader dies from not putting on extra sweater while riding bike—Mother says, 'I told you so,'" I'm not going to worry about this one.

Young eyes also see in much dimmer light than ours. We seem surprised when they do not profess great appreciation upon our turning on a light for them while they are reading "in the dark." I suggest that instead of turning the lights up, you reduce them a little each night. Either you will finally determine their "seeing threshold" or they really can read in total darkness. Think of the savings in the electric bill.

A third example of perception differences is the volume at which music must be played. A seventh grader really does require a higher volume than we do to both enjoy her music and understand the words. Maybe this need is due to the accumulated effect of our yelling at her. My only recourse has been to gradually lower my voice while telling her something important (a phone call for example), so she will be forced to reduce her music volume. My attempts thus far have failed. She seems to have no problem hearing an important "whisper" competing with 90db of "music," but when I ask her to do a chore in a loud, concise voice, she can't hear me above the roar of the moth flying through our backyard.

I can't leave this topic without mentioning sleeping habits. I'm sure her not going to bed on time or rising with the alarm in a spirited manner also falls into the classification of physical differences. If research shows physical cause for this behavior, it will undoubtedly be suppressed to prevent teenagers from justifying sleeping proclivities that seem to be designed for the sole purpose of annoying their parents.

There are two distinct camps when it comes to discussing an offspring's ability to maintain a clean room. When I joke that I have rediscovered my daughter's carpet in her bedroom, seen for the first time in several years due to a protective coating of clothes and discarded art project debris, two-thirds of the parents give me that knowing smile while the other third have no idea of what I'm talking about. Who said that life was fair?

Now when it comes to language, I am certainly dated. Passing by my seventh grader's phone session (ostensibly about homework), I noticed little on her end of the phone resembling the spoken tongue, as I know it. It is possible that the collection of guttural sounds, squeals, and various imaginative noises constitute some highly efficient code that will strain the new information highway due to its information density, but of this, I profess total ignorance and offer no advice.

I have tried here to touch on a few areas where conflicts can be avoided by realizing that the same event might result in opposite yet still correct conclusions. Why use up precious "authority points" when the outcome is of little importance?

Since my daughter will undoubtedly find out about this article as she did last time, I am giving her advance warning: "be nice or I'll embarrass you by telling your friends some dumb jokes."

—I.P. (Involved Parent trying to cope)

DAUGHTER'S REBUTTAL

Aha! I caught you again. I feel it is my obligation to respond to your somewhat confused view of how "us kids" survive in a parent's world. I will try to translate your attempt to explain how parents and children "reconcile their differences" (whatever that means). It was a great fable you referred to in the beginning, but your reflection on the story was not quite complete. Have you ever thought about how the misunderstood elephant felt? I agree with your reasoning on heat differences. Once when getting ready to go to school, Mom told me to put on an extra layer of clothes. When I questioned her request, she immediately responded, "Because it's cold outside." She could have just said, "You make me feel cold just looking at you so, even if you are miserably overheated, you have to put on a sweater so I'll be comfortable."

Likewise when I'm reading, Dad will tell me to turn on the lights so I won't go blind. If I explain that I am perfectly fine, he usually comes back with: "What do you mean? It's so dark, you'll ruin your eyes." What he truly means is: "I don't care if you can see all right or not, because I can't. Now turn on the light, so I can be comfortable even if the room is so bright that you get a headache."

To solve the music volume problem, I wear headphones a lot of the time. (But sometimes even with them on, my parents complain of the awful racket.)

My strongest protest is the matter of clean rooms. The typical teenager's room may look like any old messy room to you adults, but to us, it has its own order. When our parents tell us to clean our rooms, we are mystified and left wondering how we will ever find our things again. What you call neat I would hardly call efficient. With our system, our room never needs to be redone or straightened, because there is nothing to straighten!

There are other things that I would like to discuss, but the last line of your article caught me off guard, Dad, so I will put those particular comments aside for now.

—I.C. (Involved Child trying to cope)

2 2

BE A PARENT FIRST

I'm about to discuss something very unpopular to many of the touchy/feely types. If you are in this group, you may wish to skip this chapter altogether.

There is a popular throw pillow with an embroidered inscription something to the effect: "I'm so lucky that my daughter has grown up to become my best friend." Some mothers love to give these pillows to their daughters who subsequently display them prominently whenever the mother visits. Then daughter and mother alike will beam in its presence. The mother beams because she feels connected and the daughter beams because she thinks she needs to beam to please her mother.

I have a bit of a problem with this whole concept. I am my daughter's father and not her best friend. A daughter needs a father. A daughter needs a mother. She does not need another best friend. If she has had at least an average upbringing, odds are she has a long list of best friends but has only one mother and one father (all right, sometimes two, three, or even four mothers and/or fathers). As a caring, loving and concerned father, I think I can bring some things to our relationship that best friends can't. I think some parents push their daughters to be their best friends because they don't have any friends of their own. This is not fair to their daughters. I expect to get a great deal of flack for my opinion here, particularly from the manufacturers of the cutesy pillows. But then, I've got to stick my neck out once in a while. How about a pillow that says, "My daughter has lots of best friends but only one wonderful mom?"

I try to encourage my daughters to have friends of all ages, particularly ten years older and ten years younger. Ideally they should have a close friend in each decade of life to keep their outlook broad. Just as we receive insight from our older friends, we give guidance to our younger friends, sometimes learning a few things from them too.

It was a thirteen-year-old girl, Shellie G, who provided me with one of my most valuable life lessons. I was thirty-two at the time and the swim coach of about thirty-five kids ranging from six through seventeen. This was a unique challenge since I had never coached before and also since my coaching took place on Kwajalein, an island twenty-three hundred miles from the nearest potential competing team. Despite all my efforts I could not get through to Shellie. She never seemed happy about what we were doing in practice no matter how hard I tried to accommodate her.

Then one day she confronted me: "Lynn. Stop! It's not you. It's me. I'm even taking medication for my mood problems."

I couldn't get through to her but she sure got through to me. She stopped me in my tracks. She made me realize in no uncertain terms that when you really try hard with someone and just can't get through, it's no longer your problem—it's theirs.

We can't help everyone and need to draw a line at some point and move on. We have only so many help-a-trons in our life's purse and need to spend them wisely, lest we slip into unhealthy codependences. Gurus are teachers yet there is nothing written about how old they must be, how long they must teach, or even if we need to like them. I will always be grateful to Shellie, my thirteen-year-old two-minute guru.

Parents shivering in a cold late November rain watching their daughters play the last soccer game of the season know the true meaning of Thanksgiving: – "THANK GOD SOCCER SEASON IS FINALLY OVER!"

2 3

SWIM COACH

When I returned to Kwajalein as a bachelor for my third and final tour, I kept in shape by swimming laps regularly in the bachelor's pool. One evening, I was approached by another swimmer with the following proposition:

"I've been watching you on and off for the last month. You're really an accomplished swimmer. Did you ever compete and at what level?"

"I swam in high school and three years in college until I couldn't afford the time it took from my school work."

"How good were you?"

"I was captain of the freshman swim team and held a few school records."

"Any certifications?"

"Certified to teach swimming and to work as a lifeguard by the Red Cross."

"Great. How would you like to be my assistant swim coach to the kids here on the island? We meet at 5:30 every night at the dependents' pool. I really could use some help. Working with this group is much more than one person can handle."

I explained to him I was out of date and knew nothing about modern coaching techniques. But I did understand kids pretty well, with three daughters back in Minnesota all of them high-level competitive swimmers.

He assured me that that was more then enough. "I'll show you the ropes about coaching these kids so don't worry about a thing. I've been doing this for over twenty years now. Just show up Monday at 5:30."

"OK, I'll be there."

Monday, 5:35 p.m. Twenty-five or so kids are demonstrating levels of hyperactivity I've never witnessed before. The lifeguard approaches.

"Are you Lynn Jacobson?"

"Yeah. I'm supposed to meet Bob here. Have you seen him?"

"No, but he did leave you a message."

"What was it?"

"He called this morning to tell you he's been kicked off the island for drinking, so you're now the new head coach." He added, "And he wished you good luck."

"Where is he now?"

"Probably halfway back to Hawaii."

Conversations over the next forty-three seconds:

"What do you want us to do now, Mr. Jacobson?" "Yeah what?" "Can we get in the water now?" "I have to go to the bathroom." "My mother said I have to leave early." "I'm cold." "Do we have to swim with the big kids?" "I don't know how to swim." "I have to go to the bathroom." "My sister asked me to tell you she'll be late." "Where do I sign up my son?" "Do I have to put my face in the water?" "I don't want to get my hair wet." "I'm cold." "I have to go to the bathroom." "When is swim team over?" "I won't be able to come Thursday." "Where do I put my towel?"

Trial by fire (actually water) or, as they say, "On-the-Job Training" but with no trainers.

"OK, everybody. Line up by height!" That was the first thing I could think of to stall the swarm until I figured out what to do next. Fortunately it took those height-estimation-challenged kids nearly three minutes to figure out how to order themselves by height. For the next year we always began every swim team practice (and birthday games) with what was to become my trademark, "OK, everyone, line up by height!"

I was pretty much winging it from there. I relied heavily on various relay competitions and chose teams from the height-oriented-line counting off 1, 2, 3, 4, 4, 3, 2, 1, 1, 2, 3, 4, 4, 3, 2, 1, etc. as I walked down the line tapping heads to select four nearly equal relay teams.

I threw in free private lessons on Saturdays and Sundays to get as many kids up to speed as quickly as possible. After a few months, the U.S. Army, who ran the island, decided to shut me down as they had no take on my credentials. They didn't want the liability associated with having some strange unqualified person teaching the island's kids swimming. And, as I was charging each kid's parents $30 per month for my efforts, the army decided this was illegal under their private enterprise guidelines.

The protests were swift and strong from kids and parents alike. The kids loved their swim team, as did their parents. The army, caught off guard, had no choice but to back down, as they realized just how unpopular their original decision was. The army was trying to win "love and respect," and this move was clearly counter to their goals (it did help my cause that several of the highest-ranking civilians on the island had kids on my team). The next week we were up and running with "Line up by height!" ringing out again.

"Line up by height!" For a change I put all the big kids on one relay team and all the little kids on the other relay team.

"No fair!" was the unanimous chorus of the small-fries. They were in total revolt. My popularity suddenly dropped from a high 9 to a low 2 with this preteen group.

"OK, we are going to have a relay – big kids against little kids."

"No fair!" resounded the small-fries again.

"Each swimmer is to swim with a washcloth and hand it off to their relay teammate when they reach the end of the pool."

"No fair!" repeated the small-fry Greek Chorus.

"OK, little team. Here is your washcloth."

"No fair!" Again, their vehement response.

"OK, big team here is your washcloth."

"No fair!" shouted the *big* fries.

"Fair! Fair! Fair!" countered the suddenly delighted small-fries.

"Oh. I am so sorry. Did I neglect to tell the big team that I ran out of washcloths so I'll have to give you an oversized beach towel instead? Oh well. That shouldn't pose much of a problem."

Anyone who has ever tried to swim with a saturated beach towel versus a washcloth can appreciate how this substitution leveled the playing field.

I'm so mean—I love it.

By the way. The big team got very innovative in developing clever ways to transport their two-thousand-pound saturated towel to each end of the pool and actually won, but only by inches. It was all very exciting, and everyone had a story to tell at the dinner table that evening.

The swim team was a success for everyone. A win-win-win situation. Thirty-five kids became accomplished swimmers, their parents were pleased with their exercise and newly acquired skills, and I earned some extra spending money and gained access to numerous well-supplied dinner tables.

I also received five marriage proposals: four from nine-year-olds and one from Kirsten, an eight-year-old with one of the biggest smiles I'd ever seen. Actually she initially asked, "Will you marry my mother?"

"That would be very nice but what would your father say?"

"Oh, yeah. OK. Then will you marry me?"

I explained to all five that they were a bit young right at that time but if they would ask me again in fifteen years I would certainly give their offers serious consideration. They all promised they would wait, but none of them did. Lisa D., Debby J., Theresa P., Kirsten S., Allison M.—I know I forgot most of your names but you will always be part of my life. I still love you all.

Contrary to my daughters' assertion, I can find no scientific research to substantiate their claim that homework causes serious brain damage.

2 4

More "Mean"

If It Worked The First Time...

D2 had joined the four of us, D4, D5, MFW and moi, on our vacation to the Big Island, Hawaii. We had had a great week playing in the sun and were about to head back to the airport to catch our flight home. We sent D4 and D5 for one last potty stop, checked out of our unit, loaded the car and needed only for D2 to join us to be off for the airport. But as luck would have it for this attractive eighteen-year-old young beauty, she had finally met a young man on the beach after a week of being boy-less. Their conversation was going extremely well and he showed considerable interest in her (as he should have), so she was reluctant to break off her first respite from a week of severe boy-deprivation.

"Where is D2? It's time to leave."

D4 to the rescue. My "Favorite Partner in Mean" and I discussed the problem and developed our plan.

The only thing that worried me while formulating our plan of attack was that, through my tutelage, my daughters were developing some rather potent "how to be mean" skills. It further occurred to me that these maturing mean skills could come back to haunt me in the not too distant future. The best students tend to surpass their masters.

Too late to worry about that now. Our plot had been hatched and Act I of our one-act play was about to commence. While the director remained out of sight in the shadows, D4, the leading lady, ran up to D2 and her new heavily engaged companion and pleaded:

"Please, Mommy. Please! Can't you come? Baby's crying in the car!"

There is hope: The eighty-three-step five-year Post Daughter Stress Syndrome Recovery Program (PDSSRP) for multi-daughtered fathers has finally been funded.

2 5

FIVE RULES FOR RAISING DAUGHTERS

My experience has taught me that there are five important tenets required to properly raise daughters or, in actuality, to help them raise themselves. After we take care of five thousand or so diapers per kid (twenty-five thousand for me in total), it's pretty much out of our hands. I look at it more as guiding and knowing when to stay out of the way rather than "raising."

The five tenets I've identified are listed below in their order of increasing difficulty. After "Love," I have not been able to discern their actual relative importance.

1) Love them. (No-brainer.)

This no-brainer tenet makes every parent's list. I would not be surprised if linguists eventually determined that this tenet is actually the origin of the term, "No-brainer." If loving your kids isn't a no-brainer, then what else could be?

2) Provide for them. (Little-brainer.)

The only uncertainties in providing for our kids are the mix and degree. Allocation among various material things (housing, clothing, food, supplies, etc.) and non-things (opportunities, experiences, lessons, travel, etc.) is a constantly evolving process.

In providing non-things for our children, the bias is to overbook them (oh, really? What a surprise!), for in the smorgasbord of life there is an infinite array of opportunities. We are afraid of overlooking anything that might enrich their lives or provide them with that extra advantage needed to achieve their (our) goals often at the expense of denying them the opportunity to acquire their own arranging/organizing life skill set. We forget that their downtime contributes to their development just as much as planned activities.

3) Make time for them. (Medium-brainer.)

When our girls were young, we constantly reassessed our career paths. Eventually we concluded that devoting more time to advance up the professional ranks would not significantly improve our lives but would siphon time/energy away from our growing family. We decided that being more careful about saving, spending, and investing would be far more effective in improving the trade-off between income and time than working longer hours.

I often had to apply a bit of subterfuge as the option of exchanging career opportunities for family time was neither understood nor appreciated by management. In fact "The Boss" would interpret such prioritizing as a lack of loyalty and devotion to "The Cause," "The Company," "The Team," or "The Whatever"—in reality, anything that didn't make him look good.

One day a high-level meeting with big mucky-mucks from Washington, scheduled to wrap up by 4:00 p.m., was clearly going to run well into the evening. I left shortly after 4:00 p.m. with "I have a dental appointment," an excuse that was not questioned by the attendees, as dental appointments are undeniably difficult to schedule. No one there would have approved my real reason for my early departure—my daughter had a swim meet. After using this excuse on numerous occasions, the consensus at work was that I had very bad teeth.

4) Listen. (Big-brainer.)

This ain't easy. Even during an adult conversation, ninety percent of our supposed "listening time" is spent thinking about what we want to say when it's our turn to talk next. If it's that difficult to listen to an adult, think how much more of a challenge it is to listen to a teenager (actually 143 times more challenging, according to my research). It takes an extra, extra effort to not only listen to what our teenagers have to say but to also give their opinions a fair evaluation without interjections of emotional responses.

One night D5, then a young woman of fifteen, arrived home at 11:00 p.m., a full hour past her 10:00 p.m. school-night curfew. Wanting to maintain my responsible parent image ("firm but fair" was the popular wisdom of the day), I felt it was important that I assert my parental authority and firmly address this infraction of our house rules.

"D5, we need to talk."

"Yeah. We sure do!"

(Oops – I didn't expect such a strong retort. This did not bode well for the cause of father authority. I think I just saw a shot fired over my bow.)

"You're late. In fact, an hour late."

"Yes, I am. I found it necessary to stay to finish my project. I should have called you but lost track of time."

"Well, what do you think we should do about your being an hour late?"

"That's easy. What **you** need to do is..."

We talked for half an hour. Instead of our coming up with what I had intended to be a suitable consequence for her transgression, she convinced me that her curfew should be raised to eleven. This was an unexpected turn of events. Her arguments, based on her demonstrated level of responsibility and her having never before caused us a major concern, were quite formidable. Whether I was just a wuss or she was right wasn't the point. The point was, I listened and I found she made sense.

The next morning, as I lay awake thinking about what had transpired the night before, I mused that what had really annoyed me wasn't the fact that D5 won the argument but the fact that she was right. Kapow! Another unsuspecting parent blindsided by a fifteen-year old.

D1, D2, and D3, all preteens (before D4 and D5 were even on the horizon) were staying with me for the summer in Colorado. As the five of us (MFW was MFG then) drove down Boulder Canyon from a day of exploring the Continental Divide, we passed an abandoned gold mine. "Stop!" shouted D3 (seven at the time), "I want to see!" I stopped and backed up to D3's "gold mine of interest" so we could all see what had excited her so much. She just sat there dumbfounded.

"D3, what's the matter? Here's your gold mine."

In a low soft voice she responded, "No one has ever done that for me before."

Sometimes listening has instant benefits.

D4 has a firmer grasp of this listening conundrum than anyone else I know.

"D4, I know you are anxious to return to your apartment in the city but I would like to talk to you for a minute first."

Pause. More pause.

"Well, OK, Daddy. But only if you promise you'll tell me later what you said."

I had never heard anyone admit up front that they probably weren't going to listen but were still willing to be polite about it. How did she get to be so candid and so smart? She had to have learned that insight from her mother.

5) Apologize. (Giant-brainer. From my observations of how seldom parents apologize to their kids, especially the fathers, it's gotta take a giant brain to figure this one out.)

This trait seems to be missing from most parents' skill set. Somehow, parents interpret the need to apologize to their kids a sign of weakness or at least a confession that perhaps we aren't as smart as we'd like to pretend to be—and we can't have that. All children put their parents on a pedestal (sometimes up to eight feet high), which is normal. I try to keep the pedestal my Ds put me on to less than six inches high so when I fall, and at some point all parents do fall, I won't plummet too far and get hurt. Apologizing to your kids when you are wrong helps to keep the pedestal's height under control and teaches them it's OK to be wrong and to apologize when appropriate. (D5 pointed out that once a daughter understands the ramifications of a father's timely apology and the comfort it can sometimes provide, she can't help but raise the height of the pedestal even more.)

I've learned from work experience that anyone who won't apologize or admit an error is not to be trusted. These coworkers will often fudge unfavorable data, withhold valuable information, and avoid stepping up to the plate when needed. The same applies to people outside of the workplace.

Where better for a child to learn to apologize if not at home (and whether anyone admits it or not, from their most important role model)? However, every apology must be legitimate, for a series of meaningless apologies is just bad form. A series of: "I'm sorry, I'm sorry, I'm sorry" can get to be a real drag after a while (unless it's from your wife but then—oh, never mind, that's a total fantasy anyway).

It was 9:00 p.m. on a Thursday night when D5 casually mentioned:

"I've got to write a paper for my physics class."

"Oh, that's interesting. What's the subject?"

"It's supposed to be an original story illustrating two effects of the special theory of relativity."

"Hmm. That's a fascinating topic. And how far along are you?"

"Ah, not very."

"Does 'not very' actually mean you haven't started?"

"Well, sort of."

"Does 'sort of' mean 'not at all'?"

"Well, yes."

"Hmm, I see. And just how important is this physics paper?"

"Thirty percent of the grade."

"And when is it due?"

"Tomorrow."

"I see. At four in the afternoon?"

"No, at nine in the morning."

"How long have you known about this paper?

"Awhile."

"Does awhile mean a week or several months?"

"Two months."

"I see. Are you implying you would like a tiny bit of help here?"

"Yes."

"Well, I guess that can be arranged."

All the ingredients were there to motivate me to launch into a long parental lecture about communication, planning, keeping up on homework, and responsibility. I resisted, however, and took a more active path. Part of my philosophy is to fix a problem first and worry about its cause later.

We discussed the task at hand and what concepts were to be included in her paper. Then we discussed possible story lines that would address the required relativistic effects. From our discussion she decided to describe a Thanksgiving dinner where all the guests arrived three hours before the turkey would be ready to eat. The host took her guests on a ride at nearly the speed of light so that when they returned ten minutes later (according to the guests' watches), the turkey had actually cooked for an additional three hours.

This productive beginning was then rewarded by the writing team's consumption of a couple ice-cream bars to gain extra brain power and extra endurance. I stayed up with her until 3:00 a.m. when she finally raised her head and announced, "I'm done." I did not write any part of her paper but by responding to her every-five-minute questions, was able to help her compress a forty-hour effort into a six-hour effort and, if I may say so myself, saved the day. I am not one of those parents who insist their child suffer the consequences of their actions when the error is relatively minor and the consequence so grave. Besides, a little father-daughter teamwork can be a good thing once in a while.

"Now that you have finished, may I read it?"

"No."

"Why not?"

"'Cause you'll want me to change something."

"But you owe it to me. I stayed up until 3:00 a.m. with you, so you should at least let me see how it turned out."

"No. I'm tired and want to go to bed."

I was hurt and felt unappreciated. I thought I should be entitled to read her paper after devoting six intense hours to assist her. She refused a final time and I left, shutting her door a bit more loudly than I should have.

I felt bad about slamming the door so I bought flowers for her when she came home from school the next day and *apologized*—but I also explained why I felt hurt and added, at least she owed me a "thank you."

"Thank you. Thank you."

Wow. A double "thank you." A first!

"Next time could you give me at least one more day's notice?

"OK."

Women's bodies are comprised of bone, muscle, and non-muscle. In our household, even hinting at the three-letter F-word (e.g., do these jeans make me look...) is far more dangerous than screaming the four-letter F-word.

2 6

Four-Letter Words

The focus on four-letter words, where daughters are concerned, has been misdirected to protect them from exposure to R-rated programming and street slang. From an early age our daughters have been well aware of the fact that typical users of the F-word do so because they have a very limited repertoire of adjectives and adverbs. The shock value just isn't there anymore from its overuse. So the F-word is just a generic sound filler where most of the actual meaning is conveyed in either its context or by one's vocal intonation.

When a speaker normally chooses an adjective, he is trying to select the word located in word-space that most closely approximates the specific meaning he has in mind. When the F-word is substituted instead, content is lost.

Another F-Word

Climbing Cadillac Mountain in Maine with D1 in a poorly designed (this was the '60s) backpack child carrier was both hard work and painful. But as far as D1 was concerned, her father had slacked off and was not going fast enough. FAST, Daddy, FAST! To make her point known, she would lean as far out as she could and add to my discomfort by bouncing.

Not to be outdone by her older sibling, D5 repeated this scenario as I carried her up the two thousand Tienmu Steps in Taipei. Did I mention that, as a father, I'm a SLOW learner?

FOUR-LETTER M-WORDS

Daughters bring on new challenges in the M-four-letter word arena. For example, when one daughter lost a long debate with her father (a rare event) on the definition of a particular word, she ended the debate by saying, "Anyway, it's a MUTE point."

"Aha, you mean a moot point!"

But then after she didn't answer, turned, and left the room, I realized I'd been had again—it was a mute point to her because she was done talking about it.

After becoming physically overtaxed giving my three-year-old daughter an extensive piggyback ride, I headed for the sofa (a nice four-letter word). But then, she smiled and uttered that most frightening four-letter word, "MORE. MORE, Daddy – MORE."

"Look, D5," I said to her, (then a college senior in San Diego), "I got a free timeshare in Cabo San Lucas during spring break." I instantly knew that another of the more frightening four-letter words was about to come back at me.

"MINE!"

It was later that I realized this was an inherited trait handed down from mother to daughter. After we added a closet to our home, I mistakenly thought I would share in the benefits of the additional storage until my wife wielded that same word to set me straight—"MINE."

I repeat: did I mention that, as a father and as a husband, I'm a really, really slow learner?

When dealing with daughters there are five rules.
You can't win. You can't break even. You can't get
out of the game. Everything you do to minimize
your losses fails. And for those readers who have a
strong math background, only minimax provides
some token relief.

2 7

GAMES AND PARTIES

A little creativity is often helpful when running a daughter's birthday party. It makes the whole process more fun and more memorable. One of D5's friends pleaded hysterically with her mother for permission to stay at D5's birthday party even though she was running a high fever at the time. Their original plan had been to just drop off a present. "Please, Mommy. You don't understand—this is a D5 birthday party!" She stayed.

One year we set up the whole backyard as a carnival. We uprighted the half-folded Ping-Pong table into a game of skill, made a ring toss, a beanbag throw, and a nerve game. We even had a clown and a fortune-teller (godmother of D4 and D5) from that mystical land called Ohio. We put together about a dozen booths all packed with busy short guests using handmade tickets.

NERVE GAME

The nerve game is basically nine feet of bare heavy-gauge copper wire strung three inches off a 4x8 sheet of horizontally mounted plywood. The copper wire makes numerous twists and turns as it runs from left to right. A second piece of bare copper wire (the wand held by the player) is about twelve inches long with a two-inch loop at its end. The loop encircles the nine-foot copper wire.

The object of the game is to pass the loop over all nine feet without letting it touch the strung wire. If the loop makes electrical contact with the strung wire at any time, a loud buzzer announces to the startled player and everyone within two blocks that he or she blew it.

Insulated wires complete the circuit from the loop's handle, to a 12-volt battery, a doorbell buzzer and the strung wire.

This game is very popular with both the kids (big-diameter loop) and the adults (small-diameter loop, more difficult) and requires considerable concentration and a steady hand. Every player invents his or her own special strategy on the spot and, of course, all their friends try to be as unhelpful as they can to unnerve them.

THE FORTUNE-TELLER

The fortune-teller gazes into a sixteen-inch green-glass Japanese fishing float or upturned vase to see all, know all, tell all. She murmurs incantations as she slowly weaves her hands over the mystical green orb. We had to be careful not to create too eerie an environment for the six- and seven-year-olds as they sometimes became overly entranced with the spirit of the séance. The fortune-teller had to adjust her level of seriousness to keep it fun as she revealed each client's future. We decided that with a little more practice, our fortune-teller could have given up her day job.

Here's an example of how to lighten up a young girl who is starting to get frightened:

"The green orb says you will have eighteen children and live to be 120. You will support your family by becoming the world's most famous fortune-teller."

Boys might prefer the prediction:

"You will become the world's greatest skateboarder and discover a new planet in your spare time."

ONE-LEG STAND

The absolutely simplest game, but one that is always very popular, is the one-legged, blindfolded, balancing contest. All participants are blindfolded and on "GO" try to balance on one leg for as long as possible. After fifteen or twenty-five seconds, some of the less experienced players start hopping up and down to keep their balance. After forty-five seconds most are either hopping or have to put their other foot down to terminate their try. The winners are often the less athletic ones who can last for over a minute. We find that older adults, over fifty anyway, have difficulty lasting even five seconds (try it). The adults' shorter balancing abilities delight the kids, as any contest in which kids can beat an adult is a source of joy for them. This game can be repeated at least a half dozen times before the participants become bored. It is a great way to siphon off some of their excess energy, at least for a few minutes. Prizes are a must, even if they are small.

ROPE TIE

The "Rope Tie Game" is the most fun for the adults to watch. The kids are divided into teams of four and are connected by ropes tied together with identical knots. The object of the game is to get untied before any of the other teams.

Preparation involves tying two eight-foot ropes together in their mutual centers with medium complicated knots leaving four ends radiating outward from the center. Then each of the four ends is tied around a team member's right wrist. The players are not allowed to untie the ropes from their wrists.

Upon "GO", the team members have to cooperate and figure out how to loosen the central knot and crawl through/under/ over the various expanded loops to disentangle themselves. The first team to separate into two distinct pairs is the winner. This game is great for building teamwork as all four must cooperate to succeed. Usually one or two on each team figure out a particular solution and direct the others through the steps necessary to reach their goal.

A variation of this game (for smaller parties) uses teams of two where a single rope is first tied around a vertical post then each of the two ends is connected to each team member's wrist.

Sometimes there can be a little bit of a problem with this game if you don't keep the parents informed. Can't you see one of the little participants running home and enthusiastically telling her mother, "Mommy, Mommy! Mr. Jacobson tied us all up and it was so much fun!"

Or worse. I was talking to a very conservative visitor who didn't know us very well when the two little neighbor girls popped in and asked, "Lynn, can you tie us up again?"

Just to be on the safe side, I never play the "Rope Tie Game" unless there are at least two other adults around. People are so over-sensitized these days that a simple misquote can get you into real trouble.

Dirt Sundae

This subterfuge is a great crowd pleaser if pulled off correctly but takes considerable preparation and the cooperation of the "birthday girl."

Start with a flowerpot about ten inches in diameter; run it through the dishwasher and line it with aluminum foil with excess protruding about two inches above the rim. Take a second pot about four inches in diameter containing an attention-grabbing flower and wrap its outside in aluminum foil.

Crush three or four dozen Oreo cookies to the consistency of coarse dirt. Place the smaller pot inside the larger pot and lightly pack the space between the two pots (under and around the sides) with the crushed Oreos. The end product should look exactly like a potted plant in dark rich soil.

"Time for ice cream sundaes!" An announcement always greeted with excitement—the poor little dears don't know what's coming.

When the kiddies are lost in their personal world of taste bud gratification, bring out the prepared coup de grâce "Oreo-potted plant."

Walk around with attention-grabbing gestures to register that some annoying parent is prancing around with a dumb plant attempting to divert their attention away from the only thing that matters at the moment.

Once you have their unappreciated attention, shout, "Who wants dirt topping on their sundae?" At the same time make a grand gesture of yanking the middle potted plant out of the set-up and put it aside. Scoop out some Oreos and try to persuade any of the little victims to accept "dirt" on top of their sundaes.

After unsuccessfully pushing your sundae dirt toppings, have your daughter (prearranged) yell, "I do! That really looks like super yummy dirt!"

She then eagerly accepts several small scoops full of crushed Oreo cookies, aka dirt, to the horror of her friends. After praising its flavor, have her beg for more.

"Don't be so greedy—save some dirt for your friends."

"Please?" as she devours the dirt to the amazement of those around her.

There is always at least one friend who suspects all is not as it seems. After figuring out the ruse and at the urging of the birthday girl, she samples the dirt sundae herself. Then she instinctively joins the deception and announces, "Yummm, I have to admit that's the best dirt I've ever had. I'd like some more too, please."

Gradually most catch the gist of the deception and play along. There is always that one last straggler who never quite gets it—oh well. All the birthday party attendees enjoyed telling their parents that the Jacobsons served really tasty dirt sundaes.

PARTY TIPS FOR THE SINGLE FATHER

When I was a single parent I threw D1, turning seven, and D3, turning three, a joint birthday party in Boulder, Colorado. Tight schedule. Tight budget. No help volunteered. Can't disappoint the daughters.

By adapting to the needs of the day, I carried it off to everyone's satisfaction. There were eight kids attending the party including my three. We started around one in the afternoon with games at home (my specialty) followed with opening presents. At three, we all piled into our station wagon and drove over to a virtually vacant local pizza parlor where I had previously stashed their cake. We made a horrific mess while consuming pizza, drinks, ice cream, and birthday cake. Then we walked out leaving the mess behind. No cleanup duty for this father. Exporting the messy part of the party is standard now but was new for me at the time and ideal for a single parent.

Escape (for your children and grandchildren)

In the Middle Ages some towns had "reverse days" where the nobles would serve the serfs. The lower members on the totem pole were always delighted to be on top, even knowing it wasn't real and would last but a day. Kids from three to eight are always excited whenever they think they have outsmarted an adult, even if it's only for a few minutes. All my daughters and grandchildren love the game "Escape."

Put your arms around the little one and challenge her by saying, "You can't possibly get away. There's no way because I'm holding you so tightly and I'm too smart to let you go. You just can't escape anyway. So go ahead and try but I know all you will do is cry when you fail. Cry, cry, cry, see if I care."

Of course you always leave a way out that she is convinced you are unaware of. Then while she "sneaks" free, you look at her mother and reiterate that she can't possibly get away, and she will soon cry "Waa, waa" to her mother because you have trapped her so well.

"No good crying, I'm not going to let you go."

By now she has escaped. She will next proclaim to the world with great pride that she has tricked you. It is your responsibility to not only act surprised but to demand to know how she could have possibly accomplished this amazing feat. She giggles and challenges you to a rematch, and the game begins anew. This time you alter the human prison but somehow she outsmarts you again. Sometimes I employ an overturned chair to add to the complexity and to increase the number of escape routes. My granddaughter and grandson could play this game for hours but unfortunately I tend to time out after about twenty minutes.

KWAJALEIN GAME

The community on Kwajalein in the Marshall Islands would be a most interesting place for sociologists to do their research. I'm sure there is enough material there for at least a dozen Ph.D. theses. When I was there, it appeared to be a simplified model of a typical American city with an excess of highly educated engineers and money. But several layers of social trappings and associated complexity were missing (i.e., almost no cars, no outside phones, no TVs, no home ownership, too much money, limited shopping, ocean within five hundred yards in every direction, a predominately bachelor population, a small military contingent bent on running the island and looking important, high-level security, etc.), with only the most basic aspects of life remaining.

On my last tour there, my role, when not working fifty hours a week as an engineer or teaching math at night school for the University of Hawaii, was rather unique as I was "coach" of the swim team. I mentioned earlier that I was popular enough to receive several marriage proposals from nine-year-olds, but I did not mention that the major benefit of my coaching was my being the only adult invited to all the little ones' birthday parties—at least one every month.

I'd like to think it was my winning personality but, in truth, I had developed a reputation for coming up with the best birthday party games.

The game that was most popular with the kids was "Water Balloon Head Hold." Each participant was given a slightly overfilled water balloon, which she had to hold on her head with one hand. The object was to break everyone else's balloon before they broke yours. Since birthday parties were always held at the beach in bathing suits, the game matched the hot climate perfectly. I also made sure they participated in the obligatory water balloon tosses and water balloon relays. Water balloons and Kwajalein were a perfect fit. "OK, line up by height!"

FAMILY GAMES

Some games are for family only. Our daughters' favorite game stemmed from the tradition that, for one night during each stay at a friend's cabin in the Colorado Mountains, they would be in control. MFW and I were sent to bed early by these overly strict virtual parents while they got to stay up as late as they wanted.

I'll tell you right up front—they were tough. No talking, no reading with a flashlight, only one glass of water each, and we had to ask permission to use the bathroom. They checked on us numerous times to enforce their rules.

They invented their own amusements as the cabin lacked both a TV and a radio. They worked on the giant one-thousand-piece puzzle (a fixture at the cabin), wrote plays, read, invented pastimes and just played.

The result, of course, was that it took at least two days for them to recover—but they didn't care. There was nothing pressing on our agenda and being boss for a night was worth a bit of recovery time. Our advantage, of course, was we got at least one good night's sleep.

*When in doubt, do! Make a list of the things in
life you regretted doing. Make a list of the things
in life you regretted not doing.
Which list is longer?*

2 8

Panther Tracks III, abridged

COMMUNICATION
POINT...

If one were to multiply the number of "parent types" by the
number of "kid types," it would become evident why it is so
difficult to generalize about kid/parent interactions (henceforth
referred to as kpi). This measure is particularly large with
middle school kids (Misk) whose personality traits tend to
be a bit exaggerated. So, an approach that may be successfully
applied to one kpi may be utterly disastrous when applied to
another.

We have all had friends who, benefiting from the "luck
of the draw," were blessed with a dream child. They freely
dispensed *kpi* advice based on the success of their own clearly
superior parenting approach. Then their second one arrived,
blatantly confirming the "law of averages" with a vengeance.
With frazzled nerves and destroyed confidence, they morphed
into desperate parents seeking answers.

With these disclaimers, I will now attempt to tackle "*kpi*
communication" (the diminutive c is on purpose and shows the
timidity with which I approach this subject).

I have observed that in various families, kpi communication
ranges from "a delightful hour of lively discussions after school"

to the "passing of terse notes once a week to verify that all parties still share a common abode." Behind many Misks who are charming, attentive, hardworking, and caring individuals at school stand surprised parents who have only their home experiences to guide them.

While spending the summer in Europe, my wife and her girlfriend entered a Chinese restaurant for lunch. The Chinese waiter asked for their order in Cantonese. MFW didn't understand Cantonese so answered in Mandarin with no luck. They continued their efforts to communicate by cycling through six languages. Finally she turned to her girlfriend and exclaimed, "Oh damn! I'm just too tired to put up with this #%*&@#."

"Oh!" he said, "you're an American. So am I!"

Often we are so close to successful communication without realizing it.

"I certainly want to thank you, my favorite Misk, for answering so eloquently the question I perhaps should have asked. Now, if you would be so kind, would you please answer the question I did ask?"

There are times when, in the midst of a drawn-out heated kpi discussion, we suddenly stop because we realize we are actually saying the same thing.

"Slow down, Misk; if you examine my words carefully, you will see, as strange as this seems, that I'm trying to agree with you."

"You can't agree with me, you're my father."

My Misk would make an excellent witness for the defense. No information passed her lips during dinner unless responding to a precisely worded question, which, since it is not evident what "precise" question I should ask, puts us in the twenty-questions mode.

P. "But you said you didn't have any worksheets due tomorrow."

M. "That's not a worksheet."

P. "What is it then?"

M. "It's a review sheet."

P. "Is it due tomorrow?"

M. "Not really."

P. "When should you turn it in?"

M. "Tomorrow."

P. "So you need to do it tonight?"

M. "Not really."

P. "Why not?"

M. "We can have an extra day if we need it."

P. "But you don't need an extra day."

M. "But I might."

P. "You can do it now."

M. "I was going to get something to eat."

P. "You've been eating for the last two hours."

M. "I haven't had dessert yet."

P. "What's that bowl of ice cream called?"

M. "That doesn't count."

P. "Why not?"

M. "Because I didn't have dessert yesterday, so this is yesterday's dessert."

P. "But..."

So many words, so little information. Finally, I would like to clear up a few areas of potential "Miss"-communication between my Misk and one of her favorite parents.

1. Waking you up at 7:45 (third call) on a school day is not cruel and unusual punishment.

2. Homework does not cause brain damage.

3. Having you clean your room does not constitute child abuse.

4. Snacks exceeding two hours in length are henceforth defined as meals.

5. At least twenty percent of the clothes in my closet are off limits to you (my choice).

6. Other family members are allowed to use the phone without first seeking your permission.

We parents do tend to unfairly equate a Misk's maturity with size. We expect more from a five-foot-six sixth grader than from a four-foot-ten seventh grader. The speed of the Misk's physical growth throws us off balance. We often use vocabulary that we have had years to hone and get impatient at the rookie Misk's mishandling of these same words. We find we have different interpretations of such terms as: "almost done," "just a few more minutes," "a five-minute phone call," and "I only took one bite."

My conversations with my daughter have made me realize that with her, I'm try-lingual.

Signed, I.P (Involved Parent hoping to communicate.)

COUNTERPOINT...SAY WHAT?

I mean, really, Dad, your article was very impressive, but I didn't understand it. Anyway, on to my point of view. Remember, I'm not supposed to communicate anyway. There is one thing that "Misks" have trouble with. This is the "never-ending apology." Sometimes you expect me to apologize for some totally unknown reason. There are three ways I can handle this problem.

One is to try to spare you by saying I'm sorry (not always totally honest but arguing would make it worse). Another is to rebel (which almost always backfires). The third is just to run (no good, the problem awaits your return).

Being the sweet person I am, I usually choose the first way and try to make it short. When in motion, the "never-ending apology" goes something like this:

Parent: Is there something you want to say?

Misk: I'm sorry.

Parent: For what?

Misk: For—you know.

Parent: Doesn't sound like you mean it.

Misk: Why not?

Parent: You don't sound sorry.

Misk: But I am!

Parent: Then sound like it.

Misk: I'm trying!!

Parent: I don't care for that tone of voice. What do you want to say to me for raising your voice?

Misk: I'm sorry.

Parent: For what?

Misk: For—you know.

Parent: Doesn't sound like you mean it.

Misk: But I am!

(Actually, sometimes I really am sorry).

Can I go now? I've got a lot of stuff to do.

   A Misk (Trying to communicate.)

*My brilliant daughters could talk in whole
sentences by the time they were one—although
it did take them several more months to learn to
include words.*

29

POINT OF VIEW

I was a single parent when one evening I sent my three older daughters, ages two, four and six, off to put on their PJs. D1 and D3 came back fully PJ'd but D2 was not to be seen. I yelled a mild rebuke upstairs to her for lagging behind when she appeared, crying and frustrated.

"D2, what's taking you so long?"

"I can't get my PJs on—they're out-side-in."

I could only laugh. Her wording was so fresh and just proved what a rut I was in. Is it inside out or outside in? Who cares?

Our daughters have a wonderful and creative way of expressing themselves that we absolutely adore. Then, what do we do? We teach them the "correct way" of saying something, which, of course, isn't cute. Then we kick ourselves. "Dumb, dumb, dumb." All parents can bore their friends by repeating an endless list of "cute things" their protégées have uttered when very young. Of course, my daughters were the cutest and that's coming from a totally unbiased objective parent. I just couldn't tell other parents this, for I didn't want to make them feel bad.

For the record that at this point, "cute" does count since, without "cuteness," my position as the male spousal unit could be in serious jeopardy.

The conundrum is that we spend so much time creating what we really don't want—a daughter who is ready to leave us to conquer the world.

"Wait! Wait! Don't go. You're not ready! Stay a little longer!"

Translation: "I'm the one who's not ready."

After just hitting her teen threshold, D2 flew from Boulder, Colorado, to visit us in San Francisco. When we met her, she gushed that on her flight she had eaten this great dessert called "Chocolate Mouse."

We dragged D2 around San Francisco covering most of the highlights in two days—a bit of an overload but lots of fun for her nonetheless. When a friend later asked what she liked most, she responded, "My favorite thing was Fisherman's Dwarf."

This is clearly in the genes. Thirty years later, D2 and her daughter, age seven, were driving home from an evening of trick-or-treating at D3's house and agreed to pass the time by playing one hundred questions (they moved up from playing twenty questions to one hundred questions to keep the pressure low).

D2's daughter picked animal, and D2 was slowly narrowing down the possibilities with a series of judicial questions. So far she had determined that whatever it was, it lived in the ocean and didn't have gills. D2's daughter started bouncing up and down shouting, "Can I give you a hint? Can I give you a hint?" How can a mother refuse?

"OK, give me a hint."

"It has eight testicles."

After recovering from this most useful hint, D2 thought to herself, "OK, clearly this is either four male scuba divers or a very virile male octopus."

"You should give me credit here, 'cause if I
weren't your daughter, you'd have much
less material for your book."
"True. But then if I weren't your father
you'd be normal."
She paled. She trembled. A look of horror
crossed D4's face.
"That was so mean. Please, I beg you. Don't ever
bring that possibility up again!"

3 0

PETS

"Don't cry. We'll take Hairy to the vet and maybe they can figure out what's wrong with him."

"But he hasn't eaten for a whole week. He just lays there and hardly moves at all. He's really sick. I know he's sick."

So D3, being a good mom, takes her son and his pet to the vet. They wait patiently until it's their turn. D3, a successful physician's assistant, is able to talk quite knowledgeably with the vets, so they discuss Hairy's medical history, symptoms, and treatment options.

"First, we can see Hairy is seriously dehydrated so we have to get some liquids into him right away. We'll start with an IV."

D3's son remains in the waiting room, and D3 keeps him updated every few minutes on the vets' progress. Once she sees that the two vets working on Hairy no longer need her assistance, she rejoins her son to console him as best she can. And they wait.

Nearly two hours later, one of the vets appears looking grim.

"We're so sorry. We did everything we could but we were not able to save him."

Her son took it fairly well, as he had anticipated this would probably be his pet's ultimate fate.

"How much do we owe you?" D3 was expecting a very large bill, as the two vets had worked on Hairy for so long. But what was a mother to do?

"Oh, there'll be no charge."

"No charge? I don't understand. How can there be no charge?"

"Well, you see. This was quite a new challenge for us. We've never worked on a pet tarantula before."

SEX EDUCATION

The neighbor's mature girl bunny and our teenage big boy bunny finally got together in the perfect romantic setting, our fenced backyard unencumbered by cages, not threatened by predators, oblivious to the fascinated onlookers (or perhaps I should say gawkers), free to consummate their desires. Both bunnies were very excited and showed all signs that, now that they had the chance to do what bunnies do best, they were up to the challenge. Girl bunny instinctively turned her rear toward boy bunny but poor boy bunny, being of teenager mentality, i.e., not too swift, ran around to face her and attempted to jump on her head—proof that either boy bunny was just too stupid to deserve girl bunny or Mother Nature was attempting to teach safe sex to rabbits (I think not). After half a dozen such encounters, disgusted girl bunny reverted to repelling boy bunny with thumps to the head.

All witnesses (that is all the females) were quite amused by poor boy bunny's ineptness. If this was to be a sex education class for our daughters and the neighbor's daughters, I'm afraid they didn't learn much. I suppose they could practice thumping boys on the head with their feet but other than that, the whole thing was a bust.

Personally I was rooting for boy bunny and felt great empathy for him, remembering the frustrations I felt as a young teenage boy when awakening drives I was so unprepared for snuck up on me. Poor boy bunny.

CLASSIC SCENARIO

I grew up with dogs, mostly German shepherds. We had five acres with five hundred feet of shoreline on Lake Minnetonka twenty miles west of Minneapolis. There were no neighbors within sight or earshot. My parents were never away from our house overnight except for a yearly extended January/February stint in Florida during which time my brother and I were supervised by a full-time caregiver. Having a large dog patrolling their rural property provided them with both security and companionship and suited their lifestyle and rural setting.

Many years later our lifestyle involved a lot of family travel and our residence was always in a densely populated suburb of relatively small lots. For these reasons, having a dog fit neither our lifestyle nor our environment. We satisfied the "we want a dog" demands as best we could by supplying our daughters with an assortment of small critters: a rabbit, a hamster, goldfish, a bird, a mouse, and a cat—nearly everything except for a horse or a dog.

I felt this decision was justified when a friend, after traveling for four months, returned home to discover his dog's kennel fees actually exceeded his other trip expenses.

But then, all life's plans are subject to failure – especially if daughters are involved. Consider the following classic albeit painful scenario.

1) Father is happy to have dogless home allowing him and his favorite wife to take advantage of a wide variety of travel opportunities and freedom from worrying about the care and feeding of a pet left behind. We broke open a bottle of champagne when the last of our goldfish died (a result of our water supplier changing the purifying chemicals—we forgot to write them a thank you note).

2) Daughter moves in with boyfriend and takes an apartment (second bottle of champagne opened based on illusion of financial improvement) that allows small dogs.

3) Daughter and boyfriend acquire small dog from pound. Dog is cute. Daughter's mothering instincts seem temporarily satisfied.

4) Dog is lonesome during the day while daughter and boyfriend are at work.

5) Daughter and boyfriend acquire second dog from the animal shelter (smaller than the first) as company for first dog. New dog is, in essence, the first dog's dog.

6) Daughter and boyfriend are happy. When they travel, boyfriend's parents take care of dogs.

7) Daughter and boyfriend become unhappy.

8) Daughter moves out taking smaller dog as her share of the joint property.

9) Daughter signs lease for new apartment in the heart of the city where "things are happening."

10) Apartment owner allows only cats. Daughter says 9 pound dog is a cat. Daughter's assumption that either manager can't tell the difference or a tiny dog qualifies as a cat is wrong.

11) Daughter gives dog to friend who loves dog.

12) Daughter takes back dog, reasons unknown.

13) Daughter turns down $5,000 offer for dog by ex-boyfriend's sister, being unwilling to put a price tag on a beloved. (Father thinks: "Take the money—please!")

14) Daughter requests temporary housing for dog at parents' home while she makes "other arrangements."

15) While transporting dog to parents' home, dog makes her opinion concerning this transition known by exercising all three orifices on Mother's lap.

16) Daughter visits often, takes dog for her evening walk/poop.

17) Dog sort of housebroken.

18) On third day dog eats large amount of chocolate. Has bad reaction. Vet bill total, $425. From first week expenses, projection shows total costs of caring for dog equivalent to putting another daughter through college.

19) Friends offer to keep dog (doggie summer camp) while we are away for one night.

20) Dog flunks summer camp (she soils their prized oriental rug).

21) Daughter still visits but too busy for dog walks.

22) Dog has to have heating pad in her bed. Kitchen door must be left open for dog's convenience. Chicken broth is

stocked for when dog is ill. Dog insists on occupying a lap (mostly Father's) ninety percent of the time.

23) Parents re-ask each other their standard question: "Tell me again, why was it we had children?"

24) Dog walking, vet trips, dog feeding, etc. usurp such mundane activities as checking email, working on investments, and most significantly, writing. Dog "single-pawedly" delays completion of this book by at least ~~one~~ ~~two~~ four months. Father finds typing while fingers are being licked challenging.

25) New areas of discussion. Subjects such as: "Did the long-term bond rate finally break four percent today? Who has a better chance of wining the election, McCain or Obama? Which alternative fuel holds the most promise?" are replaced by such lofty subjects as: "Did dog get a good poop out during walk? Do you think we should turn up the heating pad in dog's bed another notch? Does dog need a new outfit for her playgroups?"

26) Daughter has new boyfriend and seldom visits parents and dog. Why is this not a surprise?

27) Daughter visits twice a month. Dog goes into depression treatable only by spending several hours each day on Father's lap. Father cannot run errands or even get out of his chair to reheat his coffee for fear of disturbing dog.

28) Father must learn to type with one hand as dog's head is usually resting on the other.

29) Dog is invited to a "Doggie Cocktail Party" at Bloomingdales. Concern of the day: what should dog wear? Will it be stylish enough? Dog fails doggie musical chairs, taking ninth out of nine entries.

30) After twenty-five years of successfully navigating through the "we want a dog" obstacle course, it now appears we have a dog.

31) Dog has first Christmas with us. Father has one small stocking; dog has two large stockings.

32) After opening Christmas presents I realize dog now has a better wardrobe than I do.

33) Dog's monthly grooming/beauty shop expenses exceed mine.

34) And, as I'm sure the reader has guessed by now, dog is a **girl dog.**

FROM THE GECKO

"Waaaaa...I want my pet to sleep in my room with me."

"D1, I told you, your pet would get crushed in your bed at night."

"But she stays with me when I take a bath, almost every night. And she smiles at me all the time. She likes me."

"That's because your pet is a gecko. Geckos always look like they're smiling. In the Marshall Islands, geckos prefer to live in bathrooms (tolerated because of the prevailing rumor they eat cockroach eggs). Besides, if she came to your room, she'd miss her mommy. Now go to sleep."

"Sing me a song."

"OK. Eyes like a morning star, Cheeks like a rose..."

PET RACES

Go! The race was on. D1 and I each had two entrants that were to make one lap around the racecourse. Victory was near.

D1 had her favorite. "Come on, Shelly. You're winning. Go! Go! Go! Don't stop now. Oh, why did you stop?"

"OK, D1. Mine's gaining. Yay! Keep going, Fred. You are almost at the finish line. Oops. You're not supposed to turn around!"

As our backup entries fared no better, we had to quit. No matter how carefully the oval track was dug out in the sand and how many times we tried, hermit crabs just didn't make good racing pets.

Next D1 decided to gather all the hermit crabs she could in a pile and take them home as her special pets. She soon discovered they wouldn't cooperate in this new endeavor either.

Every Sunday D1, aged two and half, and I would head out early to explore a different part of the island (Kwajalein). This particular morning we were at a small, remote beach, learning about the world of hermit crabs, which she and her friends referred to as "tickle bugs" because they felt so funny when they walked across the palms of their hands.

When a hermit crab senses danger, it pulls into its shell to wait for what it considers an all clear. If one picks up a hermit crab and places it on the sand, it will stay put for a full two minutes before poking its head out and wandering off. If it is picked up a second time and replaced on the sand, it will hide once more but, as no danger was evident during its first disruption, only waits about sixty seconds this second time. Upon each pickup it lingers for a shorter interval before venturing out. By the fifth pickup, its wait is barely ten seconds.

D1, not being aware of this hermit crab trait, happily gathered what must have been forty hermit crabs before she noticed the first few leaving her pile. No matter. She just put them back in her stash between gathering more hermit crabs to her collection. Oops. As the pile grew and time passed, many of the hermit crabs reached their fourth and fifth gathering cycle and barely paused before beginning their escape from the pile. By the time D1 had gathered seventy-five hermit crabs, they were leaving faster than she could haul them back. The crescendo heightened. Her pace quickened. Finally when the residual was back down to thirty or so and she could see there was no hope, she sat down. She scolded the hermit crabs for not wanting to be her friends and cried. Her hermit crab harvesting career was over. No matter. There was always shell collecting. At least they don't run away.

WHO FED THE CAT?

The cat, new to the neighborhood, appeared to have been abandoned. It was friendly with everyone and demonstrated none of the traits of a common feral cat. I admonished D4 and D5 not to feed the cat for once fed, it would probably become ours.

This cat had at least a half dozen names depending on which home it had chosen to dine at that particular day. It was having prospective caregivers' audition so it could choose the residence with the most favorable permanent food service and accommodations.

About two weeks after the cat first began assessing the neighborhood, D5 spotted an empty cat-food can near our back door and blurted out, "Someone fed the cat."

"Yes. And *who* do you suppose could have done that?"

Both girls immediately launched into their best defense postures denying any such involvement.

"Look. I'm not accusing anyone, and no one is going to be blamed for anything. This is only an informational question. I just want to know, who do you think fed the cat?"

"It must have been Mommy."

"No. I can guarantee it wasn't Mommy. Now you have all the information you need. See if you can figure out who fed the cat."

Both girls relaunched their defenses.

"You are not listening to me. I don't want to know who didn't feed the cat. I want to know who you think did feed the cat."

After one last attempt to assert her innocence, D4 stopped mid-sentence, looked at me and asked, "Did you feed the cat?"

"Yes, I fed the cat. See, you did have all the information you needed, didn't you?"

So Marshmallow adopted us and became our cat. It was only after several years that we learned from our second vet that Marshmallow was an it-boy cat (our previous vet had told us Marshmallow was a girl cat). His choice to reside with us was probably based on his deciding that with so many soft touches in one household, he would never be without adequate rations or top-notch attention.

We don't seek out pets. They seek us out.

Daughter talking to best friend.
"Your dad's really funny."
"Yours is really funny, too. Problem is, I've heard
all his jokes so many times they get kinda boring."
"I feel the same way. I know, let's switch dads for a
few weeks so we can hear some fresh material."

3 1

PACKING

"OK, girls, here are three suitcases we found at the flea market. They fit our Chinooky (pet name for our mini-camper) perfectly so you each get one for the trip. Except for your coats and hiking boots, this is all the space you have. Remember, we'll be gone for twelve weeks so pack carefully."

Next day.

"OK, D1, show me what you have. You can leave the extra sweatshirt out and use the space for something else if you want. You probably need more socks."

"Good job, D2. You are a bit short on T-shirts but don't worry, we'll be buying gobs for all of you along the way. You can't go to Alaska without buying at least one T-shirt. It's against the rules."

"Ah, D3. I think we need to talk. All I see here are two pairs of underwear and twenty-six plastic horses."

"But they all have to come or they'll cry! I promised a, b, c, ... z that they all could come."

"Only one horse!"

Of course, we all knew that really meant two, one out, one hidden.

To find out who came and who stayed behind while writing this book, I called D3 at work, and without hesitation she rattled their names right off the top of her head. She also finally let me in on her long kept secret—she had actually brought three horses. The trip was in 1976, over thirty years ago.

I told D3 during our trip that I'd eventually make it up to her that so many of "her friends" were left behind, so now I'm doing just that by acknowledging them here. I'm a father of my word.

WHO CAME?

Pumpkin Pie with Whipping Cream, Man O' War and, the stowaway, Little Timmy (the runt).

WHO HAD TO STAY HOME?

Sea Star, Star, Winter Hawk, Snow Blanket, Barron, Angel, Angel's Baby, Blackie, Rebel with a Cause, Lightning, Peanut, Chick-a-pea, Blaze, Blue, Scotty, Shilo, Socks, Tonto, Black Beauty, Pork Chop, Timmy, Blizzard, and Fairytale.

KEEP IT LIGHT

"OK girls, (D4, 14 and D5, 11) keep your suitcases light. Remember we've a serious weight limit problem."

After we reached the remote mountain cabin in Colorado it occurred to me that D4's suit case seemed awfully heavy. Then, when opened, I saw it held 30 pounds of workout weights.

"D4 I told you to pack light."

"I did but not including my workout weights!"

*Telling a hover-mother "not to worry" is like
telling your wife to be logical, the president to
admit he's wrong or the Pope to advocate birth
control. It ain't going to happen.*

3 2

HOVER MOTHER

(HOVER SMOTHER MOTHER?)

When I informed D4 and D5 that I had decided to add a chapter called "Hover Mother," they both burst out laughing. D4, responding for both, explained, "Don't even bother to tell us what you write—we live it. Whatever you come up with can't possibly even come close to what we've experienced."

The following correspondence never happened but, if it had, no one who knows MFW would have questioned its authenticity:

LETTER #1

From: Mother Hover Monthly

Dear Madam,

Congratulations. You have been selected as a finalist for the first national "Hover Mother of the Year" award. You and forty-nine other national finalists will be flown to New York at our expense to compete in the final round of competition. We will contact you with additional details in a few weeks...

RESPONSE LETTER #1

From: MFW

Dear Mother Hover Monthly,

I want to thank you for selecting me for this honor but must regretfully decline. My twenty-three-year-old daughter sneezed last week and if she does come down with a cold, I'm afraid no one else would know how to take proper care of her. Also, she is so skinny and could lose too much weight if I were not home to make sure she eats properly. When she is left to her own devices, she doesn't eat enough vegetables and fruits and sometimes drinks non-organic milk. I do appreciate the honor you've bestowed upon me but I am sure you understand why I must decline. Undoubtedly there are other mothers who could easily replace me.

Thank you sincerely...

LETTER #2

From: Mother Hover Monthly

Dear Madam,

Thank you for your response to our previous letter. We are sad to report that the New York finals have to be cancelled. We misjudged the devotion of the top-ranked Hover Mothers. It turns out that forty-one of the fifty finalists have declined to attend our finals for reasons similar to your own. We overlooked the fact that Hover Mothers seldom travel if it would in the slightest way jeopardize their children's perfect well-being. We will instead, send your certificate (suitable for framing) in the mail.

Thank you again...

HM EXAMPLE #1.

MFW's tiny mother in Chicago with MFW's brother and his wife taking a quick lunch at McDonald's.

"What do you want, Mother?"

"I'd like two Big Macs."

"Are you really that hungry?"

"Oh yes, I'm famished."

After finishing half of one Big Mac,

"Ha ha. Well, it looks like I wasn't so hungry after all—I'm stuffed."

This is clearly an excellent example of an HM. Translation to the non-clued-in: "Oh my. My son is so skinny. He doesn't eat enough. If I buy two Big Macs and eat only part of one, then he'll eat the rest and at least get one good meal today."

HM EXAMPLE #2.

Husband to MFW shopping at Costco. "Why do you get a whole case of soup when you know we eat only a couple of cans a month?"

"It's on sale, and you never know. We may want more this month."

Four days later while D4 is visiting for a few hours.

"D4, we bought too much soup by accident. Why don't you take most of it home with you. It just happens to be your favorite flavor."

"Gee. Thanks, Mom."

(Oops. I just realized I'm not totally innocent here. Whenever D4 visits us, I "borrow" her car and fill her gas tank. Must be MFW's hover mother influence.)

HM Example #3.

"Why do we have to leave the party so early?"

"Oh, I just want to get home early tonight—I'm tired."

Translation: D4 said there was a 1 percent chance she would swing by for a few minutes on her way home.

HM Example #4

"Mom? Hi, Mom."

"Are you all right? I called you three times in the last hour, and you didn't pick up. I was so worried. You were supposed to be here an hour ago. Where are you?"

"I'm at the shoot like I told you so my phone's been off. I can't talk long 'cause they're all ready to go again."

"You said you'd be here at four."

"No. I said sometime between four and six, depending on how long my shoot lasts."

"But it's almost five – you should have at least called."

"I told you my phone's been off so I couldn't call and it's only twenty after four anyway—4:18 actually."

"Well, when do you think you will you get here? Are you hungry? Don't forget to bring a warm coat. It's freezing here. It's raining, too, so drive carefully."

"I'm not hungry – I'm snacking at the shoot. I should be done in about ten minutes once we start again so I'll be there around five fifteen."

"Do you have gas? You know the stations may be closed when you leave to go back so better fill up now. It's so hard to get gas in the dark. I have some leftover chicken salad, roast beef, and ham for sandwiches. Oh, and I made your favorite egg drop soup. Oh, and also, I bought two cooked chickens at Safeway you can take back with you. Oh yeah, your godmother dropped off some homemade cookies you can bring back with you too."

"Mom, I really have to get back – they're waiting for me."

"Wait, one more question! Do you want me to wash the blue shirt in your hamper?"

"Mom—really gotta go—love ya."

"Drive very carefully, and please come as soon as you can!"

(Note: Mother will refer to her daughter's driving back, going back, or returning to the city, but will never say going back "home," for in the mother's heart, home is where it has always been. Home is HOME. MFW read this sentence and says I've almost got it right. She tells me the more correct phrasing would be "home is where the mother is.")

Father and daughter having same conversation:

"Dad? Hi, Dad."

"You still plan on getting here between four and six?"

"Probably closer to six. This shoot's taking longer than I thought. Oh, and tell Mom not to worry about feeding me; I'm snacking at the shoot."

"You better eat something when you get here anyway to make your mother feel good. Plus, she's got the usual bag of food goodies for you to take home."

"Those I love."

"I'll fill your tank up when you get here while you spend some 'quality time' with your favorite mother."

"No objections. Gotta go. Love ya."

"Love you, too."

HM EXAMPLE #5

Father and mother on a cruise. Father thinks to himself, *Why am I gaining weight? I'm being very careful to keep my meal portions in the moderate range.*

Then it hits him. He's sharing every meal with a hover mother. When a hover mother dines out, her selection is strongly influenced by a little voice in her head asking, *Would this menu item make a good leftover for my daughter and will there be enough food left for her if she gets hungry tonight?*

The mere fact that she is on a cruise with her favorite husband four thousand miles from home and won't even hit land for two more days is not enough to suppress the finely honed instinct of making sure her poor undernourished daughter has enough to eat.

As a result she overloads her plate as she passes through the cafeteria line (while in the hover mother mind set). Later, near the end of her meal, she seems surprised by the remaining excess on her plate and, switching her attention to her clearly underfed husband, transfers its content to his plate accordingly.

*My baby daughters took to singing duets with me
in the shower even before they could talk. MFW
pointed out that one of us was usually off key.*

33

SONGS

All the songs a father sings to his baby daughters, especially those he either alters or makes up, remain his daughters' songs years after he has completely forgotten them himself. And if you are a really, really mean daddy like I am, you can plant little mischievous seeds that lie dormant for years until "POW!"— they pop out at a most inopportune time and wreak havoc on your poor unsuspecting daughter.

D2 and her three nineteen-year-old college roommates were exploiting their newfound freedom of being unsupervised "mature college coeds." After a few beers each, they began singing rather boisterously. I'm not sure exactly how loud they were or how long they had been at it but I do know the officials at their nearby college stadium phoned during a football game to ask them to hold it down a bit as the crowd couldn't hear the announcer over their singing.

After fourteen years of gestation, the stage was finally set, the curtain opened and action: they began singing, *Summertime.* D2's voice rang over those of her friends:

Summertime, and the living is easy.

Fish are jumping and the cotton is high.

Your momma's rich and your daddy's *incredibly* good looking,

Hush little baby...

Her girlfriends all stopped midstanza and stared directly at her. Then she stopped too with a puzzled look on her face.

"What's wrong?"

"That's not the way the song goes."

"Yes, it is."

"No, it's not. The words are, 'Your daddy's rich and your momma's good looking.' Not 'Your momma's rich and your daddy's incredibly good looking.'"

"But, but that's the way my daddy taught me!"

("Mean daddy" reputation confirmed.)

You've Got Cereal In Your Hair, Baby Boo

"You've Got Cereal in Your Hair, Baby Boo" is a duet sung by father, F, and the Baby Boo, B, to the tune of "Where have you been, Billy boy?" while the baby is being fed cereal in her high chair. Since the baby has not yet learned to talk/sing, the father is required to help her out by singing her parts as well, in falsetto—a minor inconvenience.

F   You've got cereal in your hair,
Baby Boo, Baby Boo.
You've got cereal in your hair,
Baby Boo.

B   I don't care, I don't care
That I've cereal in my hair.
So there! I'm just a Baby Boo.

F You've got cereal in your ear,
Baby Boo, Baby Boo.
You've got cereal in your ear,
Baby Boo.

B Oh dear, oh dear.
I can't hear, father dear,
'Cause I've cereal in my ear.
I'm just a Baby Boo.

F (Much more loudly)
You've got cereal in your ear,
Baby Boo, Baby Boo.
You've got cereal in your ear,
Baby Boo.

B I've no fear of cereal in my ear
See, there's no tear
From cereal in my ear.
Oh dear, you're hard to hear!
I'm just a Baby Boo.

F You've got cereal in your nose,
Baby Boo, Baby Boo.
You've got cereal in your nose,
Baby Boo.

B Heaven knows. Heaven knows,
See how it blows in my nose.
Least it's off da toes.
I'm just a Baby Boo.

F You've got cereal on your tummy,
Baby Boo, Baby Boo.
All the cereal's on your tummy,
Baby Boo.

B   Look, Mummy, I've cereal on my tummy.
Don't you think it's funny
That something that's so yummy
Stuck on my li'l tummy.
I'm just a Baby Boo.

F   Now you've cereal on your toes.
Baby Boo, Baby Boo.
You've got cereal on your toes,
Baby Boo.

B   It flows from my hair, heaven knows.
To my ear, to my nose,
To my tummy then it goes
To my little tiny toes.
Oh, I'm just a Baby Boo.

F   Your cereal's on the floor,
Baby Boo, Baby Boo.
It's now on the floor,
Baby Boo.

B   No more. No more.
Please, Daddy, I implore.
Why is it on the floor?
My ears are getting sore.
This is being such a bore.
Now I want'a go explore
And get outta da door.
I'm just a Baby Boo.
Nothing more I can do,
'Cept being a Baby Booooo.
I'm just a Baby Boo-hoo-hoo-hoo-hoo...

Father-football carry. Useful for getting from food court to diaper changing station in time.

If a daughter's birth is celebration number one,
then the last of her five thousand diapers is
celebration number two. One advantage of having
a daughter: girls are diaper free much
sooner than boys.

34

DIAPER POWER VS.
MACHO MAN

DIRTY DIAPER VERSUS MACHO MAN #1

Is a dirty diaper a WMD (Weapon of Macho Demise)?

Advertisement special: Fly five separate legs on United Airlines during the next two weeks and receive a free first-class ticket to Hawaii. I already had nine legs so I needed another eleven in very short order if I were to take my family of four to Hawaii.

As I had to fly from San Francisco to Tampa on personal business anyway, I dug out my personal copy of the Official Airline Guide and went to work.

Three intense hours later, I had figured out how to change planes four times flying east to Tampa and seven times (three time zones) returning west to San Francisco two days later.

I took the trip, earned the eleven segments, and secured four first class roundtrip tickets to Hawaii. The downside was my being served the same German chocolate cake on five occasions. The first time it was great, the second time good, the third time fair; after that, I swore off German chocolate cake for the remainder of the year.

We were off to Maui. The only problem was that our seats were not co-located. MFW and D4 were downstairs and D5 and I were seated in the upper deck of our Boeing 747. To complicate things further, D5's and my assigned seats were five rows apart.

I asked the gentleman next to me if he would mind moving up five rows so my two-year-old daughter and I might sit together. This seemed to be a reasonable request as there were virtually no differences between the two seats.

Without even looking at me, he announced he was not moving. Here was a man who knew he was important, used to getting his way, and presented himself as someone you didn't want to mess with. A Macho Man. He looked like he had been in his share of confrontations—usually the winner—and could handle anything I might try short of pulling a gun on him.

Ah. But I had a secret weapon, for I was a father. The story of the wind bragging to the sun that he was the stronger came to mind. In that story the sun proposed a contest to see who could rid a man of his coat. No matter how hard the wind tried, the man just clung more tightly to his coat. The sun won with patience by shinning on the man until he became overheated and removed the coat himself.

I didn't have to say a thing to my recalcitrant adversary. I just check D5's diaper, made a face, and said to her, "Oh no, another accident? (I used much more graphic language to get my point across.) This is going to be a long flight. Oh, I hope I brought enough diapers!" Then I reached for the diaper bag.

Poof! 1.3 seconds later the war was over and the seat secured.

Diaper 1, Macho Man 0.

DIRTY DIAPER VERSUS MACHO MAN #2

During our tours on Kwaj (nickname for Kwajalein), we flew to Hawaii via MATs (Military Air Transport), which, at the time, was the only way families could return home. Cost saving was priority #1, followed by safety, followed by security followed by... Passenger comfort came in somewhere around priority #37. We flew backward with no windows, in seats designed to discourage elective travel. The bathrooms were essentially large port-a-potties in the center of the aircraft. If they could have gotten away with it, they would have put us all under heavy sedation and stacked us neatly in the cargo hold.

We arrived in Honolulu at three in the morning totally exhausted accompanied by three daughters who had raised the bar on the definition of what "really cranky" meant. After another hour in the customs line, it was our turn to be interrogated.

Unfortunately for us, a week earlier a courier from Kwajalein got caught trying to smuggle a couple of Nikon cameras through customs in a sealed, top secret pouch. Customs was not happy about this and took to shaking down anyone coming from Kwaj. As a result, officials were all adopting the attitude, "No one is going to get through on my watch." The standard "white hat, black hat" policy had been ratcheted up a couple of notches to a new "black hat, blacker hat" policy.

We understood that customs had always employed a few plainclothes officers to wander around the waiting area evaluating prospective smugglers based on how nervous they seemed. Their misevaluation of a father who had not slept for twenty-four hours, whose back was suffering from the torture seats (at that time I would have confessed to anything), and who was shepherding daughters on the edge of total meltdown, led them to decide that I was a sure catch.

The customs agent preparing to tear me apart pointed assertively at my carry-on luggage and commanded,

"Open that one!"

"No."

Color rushed to his face. He became more alert, agitated, and animated. I was convinced he had slowly extended his hand under the counter preparing to hit "the button" that would signal a waiting "smugglers SWAT team" poised to swoop in and do their thing. I imagined he was already thinking ahead about what he would say when he received his medal of accommodation from the bureau chief for uncovering such a high-level offender.

He repeated the command with more authority:

"Open that one!"

"I will if you insist, but I think you may prefer to inspect a different bag."

Was his hand poised to hit the button?

"Oh, and why, may I ask?"

"We had a little accident on the flight and that bag has a couple of diapers overflowing with the rather unpleasant results."

"Oh. OK. Open that other one then."

Thirty seconds later we were waved through. Was it my imagination or did the customs officer whisper, "Thanks" to me as we moved on through?

Diaper 2, Macho Man 0

EVEN GRANDMOTHERS

"Oh, D4, let's check your diaper to see if it's wet."

Finger enters diaper to check on its dampness. Finger exits covered in something not very pleasant.

"Ahhhhhh!"

Grandmother runs from room to wash hand for two hours.

Moral of the story: "If you can't handle the results, don't do the test."

My new T-shirt reads: Don't bother to mug me.
I have five daughters, and they took All The
Money (the real meaning of ATM).

3 5

Panther Tracks IV

SUMMER VACATION

FATHER'S VIEW

We were fifteen days into our three-week vacation when, after a particularly trying day, I confessed to my favorite wife that I thought we really blew it this year. Our Misk (**Middle school kid**) and pre-Misk seemed to be miserable in spite of our efforts to show them an interesting and fun time. She wisely suggested that I ask them directly rather then guessing from my observations.

"We're having a wonderful time, one of our best vacations ever!"

How is it I didn't know this? Our spatial separation averaged less than eight feet and MTBC (Mean Time Between Communication) a little less than twelve minutes and yet I was totally unable to assess their sentiments. Picking a vacation that fits the needs and wishes of a family of four is never an easy task. Our goal was to plan a vacation that most Misk parents strive for: one that would be educational, interesting, different, fun, and with a little luck, conducive to creating closer family bonds.

We opted for a combination car, mountain cabin, RV trip that included a cog rail up Pike's Peak, a narrow gauge train ride from Durango to Silverton, mountain hiking, target practice with a .22 caliber rifle, swimming, sand dune climbing, and relative visiting. (OK, so we stopped at a couple of factory outlets. After all, this was our vacation, too.)

One major obstacle we encountered early in our trip was our rental car. The American automobile is fine for commuting but totally inappropriate for driving vacations. We drove through the mountains so they could see the beautiful vista but the pre-adults were in the rear seat where it's difficult to see much at all and where competing interests, munchies, books, music, munchies, drawing, fighting, munchies... were beyond our control.

To rectify this mismatch, I seriously considered sending suggestions to one of the Big Three automakers for a special family vacation car built with the following features:

1) The driving controls should be moved to the backseat to permit the parents to drive from the rear and the Misks to ride in the front. It is true this would make driving a bit more hazardous but the advantages are that the Misks would have a better view and the parents could keep their Misks under constant surveillance.

2) The entire front seat should be surrounded by a large dome window to maximize viewing opportunity and nullify the "I can't see!" argument.

3) Large beverage containers should be built into the ceiling with tubes extending down for on-demand delivery (flavor and temperature selectable through a push-button panel).

4) Computerized laser scanners should monitor the precise seat real estate assigned to each Misk/Pre-Misk passenger. Territorial transgressions would be projected automatically onto a computer display for immediate adjudication by the parents.

5) All music in the front seat should be available only through headphones plugged into an audio distribution panel that can be interrupted by the ever-loving parents when they wish to deliver a stimulating, interesting, and informative lecture. (We would never try to control their actual music selection—there's too much disagreement as to what constitutes good music.)

I did discover that the RV portion of the trip provided a better environment for a successful Misk/parent vacation. There are three primary advantages.

1) Voilà! You carry your kitchen with you. This feature alone is worth the added expense as it allows the "perpetual eating machines" access to their sustenance sources.

2) During those rare occurrences where the Misk and pre-Misk are not in total harmony, it is possible to separate them so their territorial spheres do not overlap. Also complaints, discords, and other audible irritations are greatly muffled by the time they reach the cab area.

3) It's well known that a Misk can assume 14 normal physical positions, 7 of which a parent could assume (with great difficulty) if so mandated, and 3,207 that not only would cause permanent damage if attempted by a parent but are truly painful to witness. Furthermore, it is also understood that a Misk's growth is greatly impaired if the number of these positions is restricted to less than 823 in any one day. The RV allows the Misk to assume these various positions (while reading, plugged-in, Game-boying or just daydreaming) mercifully out of the parents' view.

I do realize that some educational experiences can be pushed only so far. On one family trip it was glaciers. In a period of six weeks they ate pieces of three separate glaciers, walked on a glacier, sight-flew over twelve glaciers and observed, from various vantage points, a total of fifty glaciers. I told them, "Look, if you don't know what a glacier is by now, it's no longer my problem!

We do abide by somewhat different agendas. Upon witnessing a spectacular view, we can't help but turn to our Misks to verify that they too demonstrate a similar degree of awe. When we see their attention diverted to some book or CD, we attempt to redirect their attention long enough so, at least in our minds, we can say we showed them the event.

Parent: "Isn't that river gorge beautiful?"

Misk: (Temporarily glancing up from a book.) "Uh-huh."

Parent: "You didn't see it."

Misk: "Yes I did, you just weren't looking when I was looking."

Parent: "But there's no way you could see the river unless you lean out the train window."

Misk: (leans out the window and glances down) "Uh-huh, like, really beautiful."

Parent: "Couldn't you be a bit more enthusiastic?"

Misk: "OK. Really, really, really beautiful!"

Parent: "Thank you, I feel so much better now."

Misk: "You're welcome. Can I get back to my book now?"

When my mind begins to wander, I inadvertently divide the cost of our trip by my interpretation of how little time they actually view the "spectacular." I find the resulting hourly rates comparable to those of leasing a 747 or renting the entire San Francisco symphony.

NEXT TIME, LEAVE THE PARENTS HOME!

My vacation was actually really great. I had a lot of fun with my Walkman, magazines, and target practice (not my sister). The drawbacks were when my dad would try to make me look at some canyon or river gorge for the twentieth time. I tried to point out that he had just shown me the exact same one, but he wouldn't listen! One problem with parents is that they take twice as long to look at a sight as us kids. They can sit and gaze for hours at one waterfall, while I can look at it, feel its depth, remember it, and go back to reading my magazine—all in about five seconds. And he wonders why I seem bored!

Now that you understand my side of the story, I will go on to describe *MY* kind of vacation car.

1. A three-story car would be perfect. The first story would be the work area—in other words, for the parents. The second would be a cage for my little sister, and the third a lavish compartment for me. My level would have a door that locks from the inside.

2. It *must* have an audio system that would allow my parents to speak to me only when paged and at the same time, enable me to hear my favorite radio stations wherever we are.

3. It would, of course, have a huge screen TV and a cell phone so that I can phone-shop and talk to my friends. (The bill would not be shown to my parents until after I have bought a one-way ticket to Timbuktu.)

4. While I'm fantasizing, I'll put in a "Star Trek Transporter" to beam me out to see friends and pets or pick up something I may have left behind.

It's true that this might never come true but hey, it could happen! After all, it's my generation that will inherit and remake the world! Another problem with family vacations is the dilemma of where to go. I want to go to the Bahamas, my dad wants to go to Zabaykalsky in the USSR, Mom wants to go to Italy, and my little sister wants to go to Disney World (so, send her!)

Usually we end up going to Colorado to visit my older sisters, which is a great compromise, but once in a while, one of us eventually cons the others into going elsewhere. Two summers ago it was Alaska. It was a lot of fun, and we all actually got something out of it. Mom and Dad got to see gorgeous sights and teach us historical facts. I got to swim in the Arctic Ocean, stay up 'til the sun went down (which was never) and shop for reindeer hats. My sister got to buy baseball cards and tell her friends how we were all eaten alive by bloodsucking mosquitoes.

During our trips I learn a lot more than Dad thinks I do. Besides learning historical facts, seeing bizarre yet natural occurrences and having once-in-a-lifetime experiences, I have learned how to make reading the latest *YM* magazine educational (adapted to my needs of course). For instance, "How to Use Snow for Facials" or "Ten Exercises to Try While Looking at River Gorges" or "Latest Hiking Beauty Tips from the Experts."

So when the matter of vacations comes around next time, my dilemma is: will I go with my family again? I guess I'll have to after all since, without me, what would a vacation be like?

—Misk

If we can't find a good home for them, they will have to be put down.

3 6

THE CAPER

It wasn't necessary for D2 to lower her voice, as only her family of four could hear her anyway. But conspirators tend to hush automatically as an acquired survival skill.

"OK, Lauren, your pants are good but you will have to change your shirt. Remember you have to dress all in black like the rest of us. You want to be completely invisible so we won't be spotted."

"What about our faces?"

"Don't worry; we have camouflage face paint for that."

They had planned the caper for two days now. They dressed the little ones in their best clothes including stud earrings for Helga and, of course, Freddy had to have his pacifier. It wasn't that we didn't want to keep Freddy and Helga, it's just that there were too many in the family and some just had to be sent out to good homes where they would be appreciated. Yet the conspirators knew that if they asked their neighbors directly, they would most likely be met with polite but firm "no"s.

"OK, let's go."

"Wait. I haven't finished curling Helga's hair and Freddy still doesn't have his new jacket on. Doesn't he look nice? Especially with his big smile."

"Yes, he looks very nice. I've finished the notes and Daddy's waiting, so let's get in the car."

They drove the half mile to their neighbor's very slowly in the dark with their lights out to be as unobtrusive as they could. While the driver remained in the car, the other three coconspirators snuck up to the front porch, making no noise and holding to the shadows whenever possible. They placed the basket holding Freddy and Helga in front of the door and did the Ding-Dong-Ditch thing. Then they hid behind some nearby bushes, close enough so they could witness the reactions of those answering the door but far enough in the event they had to make a quick exit. The father came to the door first, followed by two very curious daughters.

"Looks like one of your boyfriends dropped something off for you. I think that's his car parked down the road with its lights off."

"Look, Daddy, in the basket, and they have notes. 'Hi, my name is Freddy. Please don't judge me by my scars and rough skin. I'm really golden inside.' 'My name is Helga. I'm told I'm very sweet. I'm also told that I mix very well with other vegetables. We need a home that will appreciate us. Could you please take us in?'

"Daddy, I've never seen two zucchinis dressed so nicely before and look at Helga's beautifully curled hair. Can we keep 'em, Daddy? Huh? Can we keep 'em? Pleeeese?"

Back in the car. "OK, gang. Congratulations. We were successful in finding Freddy and Helga a good home. Now our next stop will be at the Browns' to see if we can do the same for Tommy and Brenda.

The great zucchini caper—a true story starring D2 and family. The birth of a family tradition.

"That was supposed to be a joke – right Daddy?"
"Well, yes. That was one of my little jokes."
"I agree. Very little!"

37
WHAT DO YOUR PARENTS DO?

Most kids have a minimal understanding of what their parents actually do when they "go to work." When I was growing up (I believe Alexander the Great was conquering Egypt around that time), all the main male characters portrayed in the soaps were doctors, lawyers, or architects (now they are mostly pool boys—we've come a long way). Kids today still have a narrow concept of "what people actually do." Just what does "Mommy or Daddy goes to work" mean?

Try to imagine how your child would answer the question, "What do you want to be when you grow up?" The list versus age would probably be something like this:

Age 2–4 Mommy or Daddy.

Age 5–7 Fireman, policewoman, or teacher.

Age 8–12 Doctor, professional ball player, racecar driver, nurse, camp counselor.

Age 13–16 Model, singer, rock star, nurse, or video game tester.

Age 17–22 Artist, anthropologist, scientist, one who works with disadvantaged children, video game tester, lawyer, songwriter, or beautician.

Age 23+ Video game tester, pizza delivery guy, hair stylist.

When D1 was nine, I took her to Washington, D.C., where I was presenting a math paper on Walsh Functions at the annual Walsh Function Conference. Walsh Functions are a mathematical method of breaking up signals into a specific set of fundamental components. As all papers at this conference concerned Walsh Function, our nametags included the term "Walsh Function Conference."

When I returned to our hotel room sporting my newly acquired nametag, D1 studied it for a moment, then excitedly blurted, "Now I know what you do, Daddy. You fix Walshing machines!"

MFW has great difficulty walking past a luggage store without being drawn inside to study the new features on the displayed bags. (The industry would be well advised to hire her as a consultant.) Her third weakness (after luggage and shoes, of course) is an unnatural affinity for department stores carrying handbags. If I had realized her weaknesses during our early days of courtship, I would have skipped the wine and flowers and plied her with shoes, luggage, and handbags.

One day MFW returned home claiming that one of the clerks had pulled a gun on her as she was passing the purse department and wouldn't let her leave until she purchased three bags on the spot. I became a little suspicious, as I had personally used this same excuse at least half a dozen times in the past to explain why I had spent so much time at flea markets and RV dealerships. However, I knew MFW would never prevaricate so, of course, I accepted her explanation.

As for me, my weakness is exploring cities on foot. I can sometimes disappear for the whole day probing all the main and minor streets of a "good walking city" such as London, Shanghai, or Paris. I instinctively search for streets that look interesting.

Some streets whisper to me as I approach an intersection, "Turn here, turn here. Visit me. I will show you wondrous things."

As a consequence of these strange endeavors, when someone asks D4 or D5 what their parents do, they've been known to answer, "Let's see. One of my parents is a bag lady, and the other one is a street walker."

I don't think their responses to this particular question have helped improve either their or our social standing in the community.

Illness. The night before my final exam. Ten o'clock, D3 loses her dinner all over her bedding. Comfort, clean up, put back to sleep. Eleven o'clock, D1 loses her dinner all over her bedding. Comfort, clean up, put back to sleep. Midnight, D2 emulates D3 and D1. Comfort, clean up, put back to sleep. One o'clock, D3 repeats a second time (always the overachiever). Comfort, clean up, put back to sleep. Two o'clock, fourth wash load nearly finished. Daughters sleeping peacefully. They are so beautiful. Time to study. The things parents do for love.

3 8

SINGLE FATHER

In August 1968 we rolled into Boulder in our overpacked station wagon just in time to catch the vestiges of the sunset fading behind the Flatirons, the famous Boulder rock formation. By "we", I mean the father unit and his three young daughters, two and a half, four, and six and a half, buried somewhere under a pile of sleeping bags and coats in the back, oblivious to where we were or why we were here. We had come to town so I could begin a Ph.D. program at the University of Colorado in electrical engineering. We had nowhere to stay and funds in my account sufficient to cover our expenses for no more than six months.

Ready or not, Boulder, here we come!

We hit the ground running with the help of my MIT freshman roommate and family, the head of the electrical engineering department, and the good folks of Boulder; ergo we survived, thrived, and were happy. I was father, mother, student, cook, maid, tutor, chauffeur, storyteller, and the girls' primary source of entertainment. I did nothing heroic or even anything particularly unusual but did gather some experiences worth noting.

"D2, you said you'd let me take a nap. Why are you crying?"

"D3 took a toy away from me!"

"D2, you are two inches taller than she is, ten pounds heavier, and nearly two years older. Go take it back."

Pause. Crying stopped. Thinking. More pause.

"Well, D3 is a very tough little girl!"

My God, she's right. I got up and took the toy back. Sometimes you have to listen when your first instinct tells you otherwise.

Pancakes at the local pancake house were plentiful and very cheap but orange juice was not. In fact, the cost of orange juice exceeded that of the pancakes. Solution for a poor family of four trying to get by: each D was given two glasses of OJ to drink before leaving home to begin our pancake foray and only water at the restaurant. This cost-saving scenario was often repeated over the next few years whenever we took long car trips.

To this day D1, now in her forties and financially secure, still drinks her orange juice before heading for breakfast and encourages her children to do the same.

Being as busy as we were just trying to satisfy our daily needs on a limited budget and an even more limited schedule meant a lot of turkey potpies, TV dinners, canned spaghetti and the standard, macaroni and cheese. I felt it was important to occasionally squeeze in a break from our rather conservative kid fare by coming up with a few alternatives that seemed exotic. In truth they were both simple and quick.

Bachelor roast: mold aluminum foil into a bowl shape. Place into a roasting pan. Place a three-pound roast in its center. Empty one can of cream of mushroom soup over the roast. Fold foil over roast to totally seal in the concentrated soup. Place in oven at 325 degrees for about two hours. Go away. When you return, you not only have a great roast dinner but you also have self-made gravy to boot. I never could actually make gravy but I got pretty good at faking it. Our roasts were usually good for at least three meals plus a few sandwiches. In lieu of potatoes, we would soak bread in our warm gravy.

Homemade soup: cheat. Take off-the-shelf canned soup (split pea, tomato, or mushroom for example) and add a little wine or cooking sherry to alter its flavor. Hide the empty cans. Heat. Don't tell guests (or the kids) what you did and tell them it was homemade. Since it won't taste like anything they ever tasted out of a can, they won't be able to tell the difference. OK, sometimes I get daring (for a single father that is) and add a few chopped onions when the girls aren't looking.

Be creative with ponytails: side-by-side, top and back, three in a line. You can get by with a lot of missteps since a father isn't supposed to know how to do these things anyway. Just make sure you spend a lot of time brushing their hair both because it's good for their hair and they love their father giving them one-on-one attention. I'm afraid poor D3 suffered the most from my attempts at being creative. The beauty of ponytails (more like pony-tales in my case) is they don't take much talent and permit haircuts to be spaced further apart, helping with the budget.

Skiing was expensive but how can young girls live in Colorado and not have at least some minimum exposure to skiing? When my older girls were seven, nine, and eleven, they would join me in Colorado during their winter school breaks. We spent several days of each winter visiting the local ski area. D1 was fine exploring the slopes by herself but the younger two were good for only about an hour before "I'm cold" became their mantra. I needed a solution that addressed their wishes and kept our costs down at the same time.

Fortunately D2 and D3 had the same boot and jacket sizes. The lift tickets were designed so that they could not be removed without self-destructing to prevent skiers from sharing one ticket. This precaution of the ski resorts however, did not prevent us from switching whole wardrobes. D2 would ski with me for an hour while D3 would wait in the lodge in front of the fire. Then we would join her so D2 and D3 could switch boots, gloves and coats with lift ticket intact. D2 was then content to nurse a large hot chocolate for the next hour while D3 took her turn on the slopes (bunny hill). This switch was repeated several times until the ski day was over. Voilà. We saved on one lift ticket and one set of rental equipment which more than covered the high costs of our hot chocolate.

All this was at a time when we were on a tight budget (aphorism for poor) although we didn't really feel it—a common state for the young and for the single parent. I was both. It has always been my opinion that spending time being poor is not a problem as long as one is only visiting. Dating, which tended to be expensive, was not easy during this period but then, it didn't really seem to matter—too busy.

Even when people ask me directly, I don't mind MFW's answering for me. Her answers are usually better than the ones I would have responded with anyway. I do get out of practice though.

39

TALKING

When I'm out for a walk or in a queue waiting to make a purchase, I tend to be animated, garrulous, and quite outgoing. This has been a surprise to me as I was relatively shy right up into my mid twenties, always hesitant to enter into conversations or even talk on the phone. I finally began to hone my conversational skills as I ripened, but not in all environments. With five daughters, a mother-in-law, the girls' godmother, and a few of my wife's over-energized female friends all competing for airtime, my opportunity to contribute to any conversation is monosyllabic at best.

For a while I had a strategy that successfully addressed this problem. With the intense focus of a cat about to pounce on his prey, I would wait patiently until the family member who held the floor would take a breath. Then, with microsecond precision, I would interject a word or two. I was so proud of myself for coming up with this clever tactic. Silly me. Within a few months all of my daughters developed the ability to talk nonstop without breathing, completely negating the effectiveness of my efforts.

Occasionally when I was able to interrupt one of the speakers, they immediately regained control with "that look" that yelled, "Excuse my interrupting your interrupting me, but!"

My perception that I am severely conversationally challenged at home was confirmed shortly after we returned home from a vacation in Thailand. I lost my voice due to a throat infection— I had picked up something either in Thailand or on the long flight home. Long flights are known to be rather unhealthy.

I was rendered unable to speak for nearly a week. It wasn't until the fifth day of my involuntary loss of voice however, that anyone even noticed, and this revelation didn't become apparent to MFW until I attempted to answer her call home. I'm convinced that the real purpose of televised sports is to give the average husband an opportunity to cheer and thus exercise his vocal cords, lest they atrophy altogether in his home environment.

How can women pass the speaking baton from one to another with no perceivable time gap? No break. No interval. Not one wasted microsecond. Wow! Another mystery.

I have to admit that I have (in secret for my own protection) tagged a couple of these speakers as machine-gun mouths— disrespectful perhaps, but apropos at the time. The machine-gun mouth tags are reserved for those conversationalists (actually they tend to be monologues rather than conversations) of such intensity that I surrender all hope of participating and save my efforts for those of lesser skill, with whom I have at least a fighting chance.

We were in line trying to get a cabin upgrade on a cruise. MFW was talking to me at a high information flow rate, keeping me up to date on world affairs (her world), and giving me helpful suggestions on how to live my life. All this time one of our good friends was standing immediately behind us. MFW excused herself to use the restroom, giving me a short respite. Wrong again. Without skipping a beat, our friend immediately stepped into the gap as guest speaker and continued this most appreciated and informative dialogue. Upon my wife's return, the exchange reversed itself flawlessly. How do they do that?

I've noticed that in the past five years, the right hand of most newborn baby girls has a natural curve that was not inherent a decade ago. I have not actually seen any research on this phenomenon and have only anecdotal observations to go by.

"Doctor, doctor. Is it a boy or a girl?"

"It's coming. Ah, here are the hands. It's a girl! See her perfectly curved hand? Just right for holding a cell phone."

It's Mommy Nature at work helping to prepare all girls to connect and stay connected. Boys always develop more slowly as Mommy Nature favors girls. I figure that by the time boy babies develop the same hand characteristics, cell phones will have been replaced with implants, and once again boys will be out of date before they even leave the starting gate.

At an early age our daughters sometimes gave the wrong impression that early shyness was a permanent attribute. D5 always looked down at the floor when introduced to someone new and as a result, knew everyone by their shoes.

"Hello," she'd mutter with greeting hand extended and eyes straight down. I was beginning to believe she had aspirations of someday becoming a shoe salesperson or a shoemaker.

We got to know the telephone installer guy on a first-name basis; as soon as we added a new phone line, the daughters saturated its capacity (we considered renting him a room to cut down on his commute time). At our peak we were a nine-phone-number household. Relief didn't arrive until cell phones dominated landlines. I wonder—whatever happened to our phone guy anyway?

Neighbor: "Your three-year-old daughter kept
pointing to our cat and yelling 'Allah-Jesus.'
Are you Muslim or Christian?"
"Not to worry. She's just mispronouncing that
she has bad cat allergies."

4 0

SELECTIVE
HEARING

The selective hearing sensitivity of MFW defies all theoretical mathematic limits of detecting weak signals in noisy environments. No amount of computer processing using the most advanced software algorithms known can match her ability to filter out what she wants to hear from the background noise.

Some time ago we attended a very noisy party where MFW was deeply engrossed in conversation with a group of her boisterous friends. I was conversing with a small group of male friends in a quite remote corner one hundred yards away. I whispered the old joke, often repeated at such gatherings to aid male bonding, "If a husband is alone in the woods and says something, is he wrong?" Across the wide expanse between our respective gatherings and over the din of the party, we all heard MFW yell out, "Yes!"

Another example would be dual-conversation selectivity where, no matter how loudly I talk to attract MFW's attention while she is engaged in conversation within her group, I fail. However, if in my quiet discussion with someone else, I should happen to mention her name or refer to any part of a woman's anatomy, her head pops up, turns in my direction, and she immediately demands a replay of that portion of our conversation.

Now I'm not totally devoid of scheming skills, so I can occasionally enter into a bit of subterfuge. If I am unsuccessful at getting her attention by inserting myself into her conversation, I turn to a convenient nearby male target of opportunity, lower my voice about 20 db and describe some portion of a woman's anatomy that I find particularly pleasing. I then mention her name two or three times. This approach always works and proves to be far more effective than shouting.

As most husbands will confirm, there exists a non-reciprocal communication phenomenon between husbands and wives. If the wife does not hear her spouse say something, she very kindly explains to him that it is due to his mumbling or not speaking up. On the other hand, if he does not understand what she says, it is clearly due to his getting hard of hearing or not paying attention.

OH MY GOD. SHE ACTUALLY HEARD US.

Most fathers know that a teenage daughter's selective hearing adapts to give her the capability to block out every word directed at her, no matter how loudly it is spoken, even though she is within twenty feet (allowance, car keys, and shopping are a few of the words that have no trouble penetrating her defenses).

Father (moi), giving sixteen-year-old daughter (D4) advice on how to dress appropriately in public:

"D4, the outfit you're wearing shows too much... for that part of town and you are giving the wrong signals by..."

The father unit is often unable to differentiate whether he is talking to a wall or to his daughter. Every form of potential response from her, be it the tiniest noise or even a trace of body language, is missing (except for a barely perceptible eye rolling). The clueless father has the same feeling as the ghost portrayed in movies who tries to interact with a living friend, only to discover that she can neither see nor hear him. Every father of a teenager daughter has on more than one occasion identified with the ghost in those scenes.

Fast forward three years. Father is sitting in the corner of the kitchen working on a Sudoku. D4, back for spring break and D5 enter through the doorway together.

D4 turns, looks at how D5 is dressed and says, "D5, the outfit you're wearing shows too much ...for that part of town and you are sending the wrong signals by..."

Oh my God. She actually heard me. Disbelief, shock, miracle, surprise, blindsided and, oh, did I mention disbelief? It was word for word the lecture I had given her three years earlier.

Now I was curious. Did she actually hear my lecture and absorb it as part of her own decision process, did it continually echo around in her head in its entirety for three years until it was finally needed, or was this just a coincidence?

I choose to believe and report to the reader that she had heard me. See, there is hope, so hang in here.

God: *"Yes, my son. I will answer your three questions."*
Father: *"Oh, thank you, thank you, Lord. When*
will my daughter learn to clean her room?"
God: *"Not in your lifetime."*
Father: *"When will my daughter learn to handle money?"*
God: *"Not in her lifetime."*
Father: *"When will fathers understand their daughters?"*
God: *"Not in My lifetime."*

41
Panther Tracks V

THE PEN IS
MIGHTIER

I don't wish to minimize the concern over rising violence in U.S. schools, particularly attention given to restricting weapons on school property, but these "problems of the day" tend to capture the headlines, crowding out competing issues, albeit less dramatic, that also deserve consideration.

Whatever became of the time-tested wisdom, "The pen is mightier than the sword"? Here we focus all this attention on restricting weapons in our schools while at the same time we purposely arm our Misks with an expanded vocabulary before they are properly trained in its safe usage.

As part of our never-ending effort to enlighten our Misk/ Pre-Misks, we've begun introducing new vocabulary words during dinner, where each family member selects a new word to be included in our conversation that evening.

Big Mistake. Prior to this endeavor, our Misk considered her father difficult, her mother *narrow-minded,* and her little sister a *pain*. Now she blatantly states her father is *irascible*, her mother is *myopic* and her little sister *histrionic*. I must accept some of the blame for not pre-editing the selection of these new words (but the part of the Misk Manual addressing this problem is missing). I begin to long for the good old monosyllabic days where her overt assessments of our parental traits were either too bland or too generic to be offensive, much less taken seriously.

I am strongly motivated to recommend at the next PTA meeting that all Misks be issued "vocabulary use" learning permits that limit them to monosyllable words until they have taken a vocabulary safety course leading to proper certification. Two violations of this rule would require attending a "phrase training" course.

Teacher: "All right, class, please repeat the following sentences twenty-five times each."

1) I am done with my work. May I go to bed?

2) My dad is nice. He helps me with school.

3) My mom is smart. She likes my friends.

4) My sis is right. I was wrong.

Student response: "Aren't these sentiments excessively paraphrased and moronically biased? I find number four particularly offensive and less than palatable."

I really can't understand how my Misk has mastered so quickly those bombastic words that support her arguments when she wants her way while at the same time, she adheres to those "information free" monosyllabic words when responding to a parent's reasonable inquiry. I'm amazed by the contrast between the answers she gives us ("fine," "OK," "good," "I dunno," or the king of them all, "uh-huh") and the eloquence shown when she writes for herself.

—signed:

Polysyllablelized-traumatized Parent trying to cope

Pencils Are Even Stronger (Daughter)

First of all, I would like to inquire why, if you wish for me to use one- or two-syllable words, do you use such long and extravagant words yourself? I am quite positive that you know kids are influenced by their parents' speech habits. So if you wish me to use simpler words, I would like to see some reduction in the complexity of your elocution.

I believe that if you do, our little altercation will dissipate immediately. When I say you are irascible, I do not mean to belittle you, only to assert the obvious. After all, you often express your favorite motto: "eschew obfuscation."

Look, if you are willing to guarantee a richly compensated, highly placed, upwardly mobile employment path, perhaps as a clinical cardiological endocrinologist, which requires only a monosyllabic working vocabulary, FINE!

Otherwise, I'm sorry but I would have to continue to seek employment at our local McDonald's where you'd probably find me lecturing to the double cheeseburgers about the historical relevance of meat consumption among indigenous populations or delivering a philosophical treatise on "Do we exist only to be consumed?"

Actually, I'm kind of grateful for the ability to express myself in multi-syllable words so that I can better describe my home environment. Perhaps when I am older, I will write a *Parents of*

Misks Survival Guide, but until then, or at least the next article, remember that once again, the Phantom Misk gets the last syllable.

— signed: nice kid

Every time I would pick up D5 at middle school,
she'd panhandle me for funds to feed the snack
machine. For financial self-protection, I resorted
to wearing a T-shirt that read: "Warning. This
Parent Carries No Change."

4 2

GIVE IN EARLY
AND GIVE IN OFTEN

I know of no (rational) man who ever claimed he understood what goes on in a woman's head. This topic represents a full fifty percent of all one-liner humor I've heard. My favorite summary of this phenomenon is, "Men don't understand women, but they know it. Women don't understand men, but they don't know it." I admit that men mature far more slowly than women, if at all, but in any event, maturing should not be confused with understanding. After all, historically, in say the last few hundred thousand years, all men had to do was get the seed planted then feed and protect the results, i.e., be a good hunter-warrior. Anything over and above that is just gravy as far as most women are concerned.

I finally reached a high enough level of understanding (mantra: om, om, om, om, oh my God how did I get into this situatioooommmm) that allowed me to apply a new strategy for handling fourteen-year-old daughters (I'm a slow learner as it took living though four previous daughters' teenage-hoods to even reach this level). My providing this valuable information to the reader (particularly fathers) is by itself worth the price of this book. Here it is. Get ready. Get your highlighter out. The strategy of "How do you handle a fourteen-year-old daughter?" The answer is:

GIVE IN EARLY AND GIVE IN OFTEN

If a parent has an argument with a fourteen-year-old teenage daughter, it means a parent has an argument with a fourteen-year-old teenage daughter. That's it. Nothing else changes. You haven't changed your mind, and she hasn't changed her mind. You don't feel any better, and she certainly doesn't feel better. If you haven't done your job as a parent by the time your daughter reaches pre-teenage-hood, then there is very little you can do after that.

I'm not advising you to abandon them, although I'm sure this temptation has been considered an option on more occasions than parents are willing to admit. However, I am saying be patient, keep your expectations low, and guide, don't push, don't fight, and again, be patient. Say to yourself over and over, "Self, I am the parent. She is the daughter. I am the parent. She is the daughter. I am the parent. She is the daughter. My role is to be a parent first and friend second. I am not trying to win a popularity contest (self-interest), but I am trying to be a good parent (child's interest) even if it makes me unpopular. And remember self, if all else fails, I have the money—she doesn't."

Unforeseen consequences: D1's job (she was nine)
was to make sure that their three (D1, D2, and
D3) beds were made before going to school.
Result: D2 and D3 froze at night because
D1 wouldn't let them sleep under their
covers lest they mess up their beds.

4 3

MORE GIRL CONFUSION

She's a boy

Three-and-a-half-year-old D1 was getting her swimming lesson from her favorite father on Kwajalein at the dependent pool. She had very short hair and was wearing a boy's bathing suit. For an hour everything was going just fine (except perhaps for D1's unsuccessful attempts to drown her father, a skill she tried to perfect for several years) until a rather round seven-year-old girl showed up wearing a bikini. Excitedly pointing at D1, she shouted, "She doesn't have a top! She doesn't have a top! She doesn't have a top."

I looked at this overzealous "guardian of decency" in the eye and explained, "She's a boy."

"Oh," she said and apparently quite satisfied with my answer, calmly walked away.

This encounter was not unlike the outdated joke of sixty years ago where the prude demanded that an officer arrest a man for whistling a dirty song.

I Never Wore That

D4, just seventeen, held up a micro-nano-nano miniskirt (it may have been smaller) that her mother had worn during her own college days (I believe the material for the whole skirt could have been woven from less than two rolls of dental floss).

"This is a great skirt, Mom. Can I borrow it?"

"No!"

"But you used to wear it!"

"No. Never did. It was my roommate's."

"But you told me—"

"Never did."

"But why—?"

"Mistake. It just got mixed up with my things."

"But she—"

"I'll mail it to her when I locate her. She may still want it."

Skirt goes back into the closet where it occupies three cubic inches.

D4 at twenty-two, took a conservative turn.

"Mom. You can't wear this top without a bra."

"But I'll be wearing a solid print blouse with a sweater over it, so nothing will show."

"But what if it gets hot and you decide to take off the sweater. Then it could rain making your blouse transparent. I'll pick out something else for you to wear."

"But I'm only going to the drugstore. I'll be home in ten minutes."

"Here, wear this."

The generation gap flipped 180 degrees in five short years. Now it's my daughter who gets upset if I have a shirt button unfastened or a twisted collar.

It Was All MFW's Mother's Fault.

When MFW was budding into womanhood around twelve, her mother took her aside while shopping and said,

"Daughter. You are getting bigger and are starting to become a woman. We need to buy you a *blazier*."

MFW's mother spoke excellent English but having been raised in China, she never quite mastered English words containing an r; the "l" sound hung on for at least twenty years after coming to the United States.

"But Mom, I have a blazer."

"You do? I don't remember seeing it."

"Yeah. I have a nice blue blazer with pretty brass buttons down the front and a gold emblem sewn onto the pocket."

Mother looked a bit confused.

"When did they start putting brass buttons and pockets on blaziers?"

"It's the style now."

"Oh."

Subject dropped. Miscommunication reigned and for several more years, MFW never got around to buying her first bra.

On other occasions, when MFW's mother was very upset with MFW, she would admonish her with, "Go to your loom!"

"But, Mom, I can't."

"Why not?"

"Because I don't have a loom."

"Go to your loom. You know what I mean."

"Mom, I don't even know how to weave!"

After this dialogue was repeated a few times, it would usually degenerate into laughter, at which point her mother couldn't remember why she was upset in the first place. MFW made it through teenager-hood without ever having to "go to her loom" (or wear a "blazier") – although in retrospect, learning to weave might not have been such bad idea.

***Newsbreak**: New pool filter developed to remove testosterone from swimming pools. NASCAR buys rights for use as a racing car power additive.*

44

~~Boys Are Not the Enemy~~ ~~Most Boys Are Not the Enemy~~ Most Boys Under ~~18~~ 16 Are Not the Enemy

No matter what a parent of daughters may think, boys are not the enemy. Well maybe a few are. Well, at least most of the boys under sixteen are OK. Their cluelessness works in our favor here. What to do? I have a few suggestions that may be of help.

1) Don't be too suspicious without cause.

2) Drive your daughter and her friends whenever you get a chance. Be the dance chaperone (this suggestion is explained more fully in Chapter 10, Tips).

3) Remember, ninety-nine percent of thirteen-year-old boys are clueless. It's the seventeen-year-olds you have to worry about.

4) Love at fourteen or fifteen is real but by the next week, sometime around Wednesday, it will be history. The reason I don't believe in marrying young is because the recipe of life calls for "then cook on low heat for six years and, while stirring occasionally, slowly fold in additional ingredients as needed." Young lovers will evolve and grow but usually in different directions. The reader should know that "too young" is subject to interpretation. MFW thinks it's just under forty for our daughters but I think it's more like mid-twenties. (Yes, I know, Juliet was probably thirteen and Helen of Troy could have been even younger but look what happened to them.)

5) As their modesty grows, so does their need for privacy.

6) They will begin to distance themselves from you for a few years starting with middle school and retreat to "uncle hugs" from full hugs. Don't take offense and don't try to understand—just go with the flow and let the estrogen side of the family do its thing. There is nothing you can do about it anyway.

7) I love Suzy Orman's advice, "Fall in love, check their FICO score, then proceed." It's great advice but difficult to pass on to your daughters.

D5 and a good friend of hers decided that at thirteen, they were old enough to have their first boy/girl party provided it was chaperoned by her friend's mother. We received a panic call from the parent of one of the invited girls to the effect:

"But there will be boys there!"

"True, but these are nice, undeveloped, socially inept, thirteen-year-old boys who set the standard for what clueless is all about."

"But my daughter is too young to be with a boy."

"A sixteen-year-old, yes. A thirteen-year-old, not a problem. Granted there are pockets of thirteen-year-olds who are too advanced for today's world, but the boys attending this party just aren't in that category. Also, the mother of the girl giving the party will be chaperoning so there's really very little risk."

The mother felt better and did let her daughter attend.

The party took place and sure enough, the girls' expectations were not met. The girls played up-to-date music and wanted to dance, dance, dance, but all the boys wanted to do was to eat pizza and play video games. The girls considered the whole evening a total bust whereas the boys thought it was a great party. After all, they never did run out of pizza.

*By the time I figured out how to raise daughters I
no longer needed the information.*

4 5
BEST PLACE TO SHOP

D4 and D5 meet while shopping.

"Oh, you're shopping here today, too?"

"Yeah, I love shopping here."

"Me, too. The prices are so reasonable though the selection can sometimes be a bit limited. At least it is today."

"Yeah. I noticed there isn't much new stuff but then, what's here is pretty high quality. What did you get so far?"

"I found a great pair of beautiful red shoes. Look! They fit perfectly."

"Wow, they look nice. You must be thrilled. I searched all the shoe racks but didn't see anything nearly as cool as those. I did pick up this great blue sweater—feel how soft it is—and a couple of shirts though. They should work for me as good everyday wear."

"Those shirts look like they would go with almost anything. Do they fit?"

"A bit large, but they'll work OK until I can find something better."

"Have you been to kitchenware yet?"

"Yeah, but I didn't see very much that I didn't already have. In fact what I got last time is much better quality than what I saw today. Actually, I've been concentrating more on the canned goods section. I'm getting low and need a few extra staples. I got some cans of tuna and a pretty good assortment of soups."

"Me, too. This section seems to have improved quite a bit lately. Much more inventory than usual."

"You going to shop anywhere else before you head home?"

"I thought I'd get some more office supplies and I was checking out this new camera. Here, see? It's 8 mega-pixels, has a 5X zoom, and is so compact. Also, I'm strongly considering upgrading my printer."

"You know, in addition to the great savings, I like the fact you can always bring things back, no questions asked. Working or not."

"Yeah. This really is the best shopping around."

"Well, let's check out."

"OK."

"Bye, Mom and thanks! I'll be back to see you Wednesday."

"Oh. And I'll bring back those black shoes – I think they look better on you anyway. Do you, by any chance, have an extra black ink cartridge for the printer I borrowed last week?"

Mom appears. "Girls, are you hungry? Can I get you something to eat? I've got some fresh soup on the stove. You look so thin! And, your godmother left a new batch of chocolate chip cookies, so be sure you take some for later."

"Great, Mom. Thanks. By any chance is that the same soup that I saw in the Crock-Pot two weeks ago?"

"No. I threw that out yesterday."

"Then I'll have some."

"Oh. And Mom, can I borrow your car for a few hours? I've got some errands I gotta run before I head back to the city and I'm kinda low on gas."

"OK. By the way, has either of you girls seen my new red shoes or my new little pocket camera?"

Another little-known fact: The origin of the Home Shopping Network dates back to at least 3500 BC.

True origin of the "Home Shopping Network."

*87.3% of all dents/scrapes/scratches of a
daughter's first car occur in the first two weeks so
make sure it is at least twelve years old.*

46

GO AWAY

"Now when we get to Prince Rupert and find our cabins on the ferry, we have to figure out in advance which daughter will stay with you and which with me. I think D5 should stay with me 'cause she's the youngest and needs her mommy the most and D4 with you."

"We won't get there for another day so why decide now?"

"We should decide now so there won't be any confusion when we get there. We'll be boarding the ferry at 5:00 a.m. and we'll be too tired to think."

"You know, they may want to stay in their own cabin together."

"No way! They'd be too scared not to have us with them."

Four hours later.

"OK, D4 should stay with me 'cause she's twelve and would be more comfortable with her mommy. D5 likes staying with you anyway because you let her stay up late."

Four hours later.

"I've decided both D4 and D5 can stay with me if they want. That way they won't feel slighted and won't fight over it."

"What if they want to stay with each other?"

"I asked them about it before we left. They both really want to be with me first but understand that, depending on how big the cabins are, one of them may be staying with you. Also, they don't want to hurt your feelings."

"Look, Mommy! Look, Daddy! Look how big the boat is! This is going to be fun."

"Girls, stay with us until we get to our cabin. Then you can explore the whole ship by yourselves."

"Mr. and Mrs. Jacobson, this is your first cabin."

"Wow, Mommy! This is great!"

"Yeah, it's so cool."

"Mr. and Mrs. Jacobson, this is your second cabin."

"Oh, this is nice too."

"D4, D5, what do you think of this cabin? Girls? GIRLS? Where are they? Did they get lost? I don't see them."

"I last saw them in the other cabin."

Knock, knock, knock. "D4? D5? Are you in there?"

"Go away!" Giggle, giggle.

"Can you come out so we can talk?"

"Go away! No parents allowed!" Giggle, giggle. Explosive laughter.

So who's in charge here?

Problem resolved.

D5 learned her first words in their order
of importance while in Hawaii. Mamà and Ma
(for grandmother and mother) were one
and two followed by pool and Dadeh (later
migrating to "Duh") for her sister. Daddy
only came fifth because our cat had stayed
behind and we didn't have a dog.

47

EARLY ACADEMICS

"Go to your room and don't come out until you finish your homework."

WRONG

In general, parents are not certified experts on educating their kids. However, when they make the effort, they often do a better job than the educational institutions. This is easy to confirm by just watching the success rate of home-schooled children. Parents usually improve as they figure out how the learning process works (if their kids don't exhaust them first). Both the parent and child benefit from the parent's ability to tailor their teaching to the child's specific learning style rather than taking the one size fits all approach.

While MFW and I do not profess to be educational experts, by the time D4 and D5 came along, we began to get an inkling of what helped and what didn't help. Being overeducated probably helped us, but just as likely got in the way.

EARLY-EARLY

From day one hundred (not from day one because we were catching up on our sleep), we concentrated on the usual early-early academic preparation: playing with them, exposing them to their great new world (within a radius of about fifty feet) and singing to them. By the time they were a little over two years old, we regularly read to them, told them stories, took them to the library, and exposed them to classical music (including "Itsy Bitsy Spider Climbed up the Water Spout," of course), typical for involved parents. All we had to give up for this privilege was sleep, our own social interactions, income, cleaning, organization of the house, time alone, grooming, career advancement, and health, i.e., the usual parental trade-offs.

Education does not open doors—you have to do that yourself. It does, however, keep the doors from being locked so you can open them.

4 8

DADDY MATH I

Somewhere around the time that each daughter turned three, our early pre-academic preparation moved out of first gear. MFW worked with the girls on their alphabet with emphasis on pronunciation (P is for pool, D is for daddy, M for mommy, B for baby, TM for transcendental meditation, IPO for initial public offering, etc.) and I worked with them on their shapes (starting with circles, triangles, and squares) and numbers. Each member of the family had his or her own special letter to aid in learning additional letters. D for daddy kept losing out to D for dog so, to get any billing at all, I had to add L for Lynn as my special letter.

We leaned a whiteboard against the couch in the living room at floor level. A parental unit would sit on the floor next to the preschooler unit, side by side, and practice drawing shapes. Since daughter and parent were now at the same level, it seemed more like a joint "family fun" project than an academic lesson. MFW and I would adjust what we thought should be explored each day on the fly, depending on our daughter's attention level, her interest, and our concept of "where do we go from here." We started when D* was three and kept it up until she entered first grade.

Did you know a little kid cannot draw a triangle or square? I didn't. If you demonstrate how to draw a triangle for them, they will try to copy your example without taking the marker off the board. What is supposed to be a sharp corner becomes, to various degrees, a round corner. It took most of one lesson to get D* to pick up her marker at the end of one side of a figure and come in at the corner from another direction, making contact on the board to draw the adjoining side. This approach produced nice distinct corners.

One of our favorite early activities was for me to start with a blue marker and draw 1, 2, 3, and 4 in 15-inch letters covering the entire white board. Then D* would trace over them in green, then in red, then in yellow until each color had a turn. After showing Mommy how pretty her creations were, we repeated the process with some of the other integers. By the end of the week, D* could draw the entire set of numbers with no assistance from the parental unit.

The problem came with the erasing. Each multicolored set of numbers was an attractive work of art. I felt awful every time I erased her work to begin anew but calculated that the alternative would require $10,000 to $15,000 worth of whiteboards and the addition of two more rooms to our home to store them all. I could have marketed them at local art galleries but our overbooked schedules and limited financial resources discouraged such efforts.

After mastering her number drawings, we repeated the procedure with letters until she had mastered writing all the letters as well as the numbers—at least when they were fifteen inches high.

*New parents soon discover that they gain a lot of
weight eating their children's leftovers.*

4 9

I Don't Like It!

I don't like it! (Does this sound familiar?)

D2 was approaching four, so as a special treat to recognize this momentous milestone, I took her for a one-on-one daddy-daughter brunch at the Yukwe Yuk Officers' Club on Kwajalein (yukwe yuk in Marshallese has the same meaning as aloha in Hawaiian).

She was quite content with the food she had selected from the food line—bacon, eggs, fruit, and a couple of small cinnamon rolls, known items all within her comfort zone.

After round one, I returned to the food line and made a rather decent chocolate sundae as a special treat for her. She had never seen a chocolate sundae before and being the most cautious eater of the five declared, "I don't like it," as soon as she saw me approaching the table with this treat in hand.

"D2, this is a chocolate sundae—you'll really like it."

"I don't like it."

"I'm serious, kids really love chocolate sundaes."

"I don't like it."

"D2, I know adults always tell you how good stuff is just to get you to try something new, but I don't."

"I don't like it."

"D2, I've never lied to you. This is the first time I've ever asked you to try something new by telling you that you will like it."

"I don't like it."

"For me, open your mouth and take one bite. Then I'll leave you alone."

Her nod agreeing to open her mouth was accompanied with, "I don't like it."

Eyes shut, nose scrunched up, palms clutching the arms of the chair, her mouth reluctantly opened as she recited her mantra. The spoon of vanilla ice cream dripping in chocolate sauce slowly approached its target accompanied by the Greek chorus—

"I don't like it. I don't like it. I don't like it. I don't like it..."

Enter, contact, response. Eyes fly open. Smile takes no prisoners and captures face.

"I like it! I like it! I like it! I like it! I like it! I like it..."

She ate two.

Octopus And Giggles

Several bachelors had joined us for a day of diving and spearfishing in the Kwajalein lagoon. Although we had caught only two small fish, we more than made up for this shortcoming by capturing a medium-sized octopus. Jimmy, a Taiwanese friend who lived in Hawaii when not working remote sites for the government, volunteered to cook for us.

"I cook. You invite ten. 7:00 p.m."

We didn't hesitate, for Jimmy was by far the best cook on the island. He usually starts at four, opens his first beer ten minutes later, finishes at seven, and passes out at eight. He can "wok" a mile a minute with a can of beer super-glued to one hand. He's got the fastest spatula in the Pacific.

When we reached shore, Jimmy and one of his friends disappeared with the octopus. We called half a dozen friends and then set up for the feast.

Jimmy showed up with the octopus all cleaned, sliced, and prepped for the wok. It was delicious, of course, but one diner consumed far more than her share. D2 hit on it and thought it was ambrosia. She ate nearly a third of the octopus by herself giggling all the time. Our Hawaiian friends taught her to throw the slices straight to the back of her mouth and crush it with her molars. It crushes fairly easily, but it is difficult to chew off a piece with one's front teeth. The final outcome was a full tummy of octopus and a full face of giggles for D2. And this is a girl who wouldn't try a chocolate sundae. Go figure.

While Jimmy was still standing, I had to ask, "Jimmy. I thought an octopus was very difficult to clean. All that pounding and the problems with removing the slime?"

He smiled, lowered his voice and whispered, "No. Octopus not difficult to clean. Washing machine difficult to clean afterwards."

Jimmy had run the octopus through the washing machine for six complete cycles (sans soap of course). I think this is a secret ancient Hawaiian technique for preparing octopus never divulged to the missionaries.

DRUNKEN SHRIMP

We were guests at a banquet held in MFW's honor by her niece, the president of a major bank in Sheng Yang, China.

MFW mischievously told her niece that D2, who had joined us on that trip and was then in her late thirties, loved drunken shrimp, so dish after dish of this delicacy kept appearing in front of hapless D2. Drunken shrimp arrive at the table very much alive, swimming around in a bowl of wine. The diner is expected to scoop out a jumping shrimp, cook it in hot oil on the table and then—down it goes.

D2, the girl who wouldn't eat a chocolate sundae, kept glaring at MFW with the expression, "I'm going to get you for this."

The real reason parents have their daughter wear
braces is to postpone their kissing boys,
at least for a few months.

5 0

Panther Tracks VI

KEEP YOUR DISTANCE!

Growing bored with the perceived slowness of her parents' disengagement from a brief social visit, my Misk requested the car keys so she could amuse herself by listening to music on the car radio. Upon my arrival she had this puzzled look on her face.

Misk: (Staring at the radio.) "Who tuned the radio to this station?"

Parent: "I did."

Misk: "You mean you listen to this station, too?"

Parent: "Yes, I like the music."

From her sullen look I knew I had just committed a serious blunder and in fact, from that day on, I never again heard her listening to that station. It's OK to like two or three of the same songs as your parents, but to share a whole station, that's just too much!

Perhaps I've discovered something new here. Instead of trying to dissuade her from a particularly poor choice, I should wholeheartedly embrace those items on the top of my "poor taste list" to hasten their being rejected as too adult and therefore of questionable value.

Recently, when picking my Misk up from school, I made the error of getting out of my car to greet her (conforming to an adult form of showing respect). However, this time, while threading my way through that quagmire of Misk/parent public etiquette, I had gone astray. I somehow missed the rule about not being seen with an offspring at school. If Misks had any control over the matter, all vehicles used to fetch Misks after school would have fully tinted windows obscuring the fact that there may be a real person (or even a parent) in the vicinity.

It would be of great assistance for us uninformed parents (Misk-informationally challenged) if the Misks would generate an operator's manual to guide our behavior in their presence. The writing of this manual would make an excellent class project. Each parent could receive a copy on the first day of school (or alternately be required to attend a seminar) so they could avoid serious transgressions or, at a minimum, be aware of their crime. Perhaps passing a written test on this subject should be a prerequisite for parents to receive campus visiting privileges. My main concern is that the rules compiled in such a manual would undoubtedly change too rapidly to be put to paper. Aha! Another use of email. Just think, each morning you could log in to determine the "Rules du jour." I can see it now:

Parent: (while opening the car door) "Hi!"

Misk: "Hi."

Parent: "How did school go today? Anything really interesting take place in class?"

Misk: "If you turn to page 73, paragraph 5a, of your parent manual, you will see that all inquiries into my school activities must wait until I have been properly snacked and beveraged and had forty-five minutes of socializing on the phone to unwind.

Any more serious errors like this, and you may be subject to a refresher course."

I have good news for all you other Misk fathers. Upon my breaking one of these Misk/parent rules during a Misk-after-school-retrieval mission, she lamented, "Why couldn't I have a normal father like all the other kids?"

There, you have it from an authority. You are all normal fathers, a parental state that perpetually escapes my near-term grasp.

Signed,

A near normal parent trying to follow the rules.

OK, DAD...

Let me get this straight first. That radio station was getting old! That's why I handed it over to you. Now that I've gotten that out of the way, I completely agree with your idea of a Misk "guidebook" of some sort, and it'd be much better on email! That way, I could basically control how my mom and dad would act toward me. The book would have to have some sort of limits, for instance: nothing illegal, nothing that would permanently remove your parents, your sister, or brother from your life.

I already know what some of the rules would be.

1. Parents are not to set foot on school campus during school hours or school activities (without written permission signed by the Misk) and must wait an extra half hour after activities have subsided to avoid being seen by other Misks (unless the parent takes the following necessary precautions: hires a limo and wears a chauffeur suit with dark glasses).

2. Under no circumstances are parents allowed to listen to or comment on conversations between a Misk and her friends

due to the parents' inability to appreciate the high level of intellectual interaction taking place.

3. Parents are not allowed to compare their own Misk to their Misk's friends. For instance "See how Susie gets her homework done three days early and gets all As?" Of course the fact that Susie has no life and no personality has failed to occur to your parental mind.

4. Parents will not point out inconsistencies such as: "Even though it's midnight, I'm not tired and I really don't need much sleep" vs. "I don't care if it is ten in the morning — I need my beauty sleep."

5. Parents must not submit ridiculous articles (embarrassing their Misk to the max) to the *Panther Tracks.*

6. This is so much fun. I'm sure I could come up with another hundred rules but I'm afraid my dad would pull the plug before I got much further.

If any of the above rules are broken, necessary actions will be taken. Judgment of whether or not a rule was broken will be left entirely up to the Misk.

—Gotta B. Me

Nearly every parent, while trying to help
his or her child with math homework,
has heard the complaint,
"I don't want to know how to do it. I just
want the answer."

5 1

DADDY MATH II

After D* was comfortable drawing the numbers 1–10 on our whiteboard, we advanced to the concept that each number actually represented a quantity (abstract) and not a thing (noun) or an action (verb). Shifting the emphasis to "how many" from "what is being counted" involves finding a one-to-one correspondence between each "number" and the quantity it represents. Getting a little one to grasp this abstract relationship takes patience, for it's a radical leap in her thought process.

In this pursuit, I wrote numbers, 1, 2, 3, and 4 (later higher values) vertically on the left side of the whiteboard and to the right of this column, drew pictures of four balloons, two trees, three stick figures and one star. Then I asked D* to trace a line from each number symbol to the drawn group that represented that particular quantity. I varied the order of the drawn groups (and colors, too, to make it more fun) so she really did have to search to find matching correspondences. Each daughter added criteria I hadn't anticipated. D5, for example, wanted to trace a number to its corresponding group without crossing a previous tracing. This led to some rather circuitous paths but then they seemed to enjoy the challenge.

By the time we reached the entire 1 through 9 range, my figure drawings took most of the time, but D* would wait patiently, for she relished the attention if not the "game". I'd like to be able to report that my drawings improved with time but in truth, my stick drawings of little people were just as bad at the end of these math lessons as they were at the beginning. Fortunately, D* would not reach the art-critic stage for another year.

Moving on to simple addition and eventually subtraction was a natural progression from the one-to-one correspondence lessons. We also worked on all the basic shapes, spending most of our time on "what comprises a circle." We used string tied to the center point to show the circle equal-distance property (radius and diameter) and learned to identify the basic parts of the circle. By using string marked in radii lengths, she even grasped the concept that the circumference of a circle was a little longer than three diameters.

By the time D* finished first grade, she knew her multiplication tables. We used flash cards and a few tricks to reinforce her learning the more difficult pairs. Example: 7×8 is 56. Reordering the numbers gives 5678. 7×7 rhymes with heaven and in San Francisco heaven is the '49ers football team. And the micro poem: 6 times 2 is 1, 2; 6 times 4 is 2, 4; 6 times 8 is 4, 8. We spent a lot of time on the powers of two (see the "You Embarrassed Me" chapter) and the squares of 11 though 16.

SIBLING INFLUENCE

One evening D4 (just short of six) and I were working Daddy Math on the whiteboard when D5, then barely three, burst into the room looking most determined and very upset. She had just finished her shower and was wrapped in several large towels, more than doubling her apparent size. She studied D4 and her favorite daddy working together at the whiteboard, stamped her foot spraying us with a fine mist, not unlike a dog shaking off excess water, and demanded, "I want my math lesson, and I *want it now!*"

D4 sprang to her feet and went poof, and I erased the board to set up for lesson one. We were all experienced enough to know that, in this household, no one messes with D5 when she is that determined.

Nontraditional Math

"OK, D4, D5, it's time for 'Daddy Math.'"

"But it's Saturday. We wanted to go outside and play."

"Sorry, 'Daddy Math' first. Go put on your sneakers."

"Wheeeee!"

So why the enthusiasm? My understanding is that girls seem to excel (or a least keep up with) boys in math until about the fifth grade. Even adjusting for the fact that some girls, knowingly or unknowingly, dumb themselves down to be more popular with boys, and that some teachers, unconsciously or consciously, feel that girls don't need as much math, they still fall behind. (We had a sixth-grade teacher who explained to a friend that girls don't need as much math as boys so she wasn't going to waste a fast-track math slot on his daughter.)

I feel that one reason some girls fall behind is that they don't spend enough time living in three dimensions. When a boy climbs a tree, he often has to reach around the tree beyond his sight to find a handhold. He can't perform this task successfully unless he can visualize in three dimensions. Girls are at a disadvantage when they are discouraged from climbing trees, thus "Saturday Daddy Math" loosely translates into, "Tree Climbing Math."

I searched various nearby parks to find climbing trees with a degree of climbing difficulty that matched or slightly exceeded our daughters' abilities. During Daddy Math, they would have a go at climbing them. It's doubtful that they acquired as much climbing skill as a typical high-energy boy, but they did gain enough experience to improve their feel for the three-dimensional world.

There is no real way to measure the advantages they gained from these adventures, but we had a good time. D5 later become an all-American and a world-ranked fencer, which I feel was partly a result of the experience she garnered from these early climbing forays.

Just as telling stories augments reading, playing puzzle games augments math. Often when I put a five-year-old daughter to bed, I would spend a few minutes asking questions such as: "I'm thinking of two numbers. If I add them I get 14. If I subtract them I get 4. What are they?"

On other occasions I would try to trick them by asking, "What's the largest number on this piece of paper?"

"Six.

"Why not the nine?"

"Because the six is two inches high, and the nine is only one inch high. And two inches is larger than one inch."

They knew to question every question—to look at every problem in many ways at once.

And what makes you think she's overbooked?

A common belief: women gain half a shoe size
with each pregnancy. Lesser-known fact:
men lose three quarters of an inch in
height with each daughter. I used to be 6'2". Now,
I'm barely over 5'10".

5 2
HOW THEY LEARN

I really didn't teach my daughters how to read. They took the lead soon after I set the stage. I just had to be at the right place at the right time with the right tools. My task was to be sensitive enough to watch their progress, provide the right environment, encourage and nurture their interest, and step in when I could add something of value.

Reading to them and telling them stories at night or during long drives instilled in them the love of books from a very young age. MFW worked with their letters and associated sounds to give them the tools. I just happened to be there to carry on to the next level what she had begun.

I've heard many arguments about the proper way to teach children to read, which boil down into the two camps of phonetics and sight-reading. Between third and fourth grade, I transferred from a school that emphasized learning to read in fourth grade to one that emphasized learning to read in third grade. My timing couldn't have been worse, and I missed both. My initial training was with the phonetics method but since I didn't pronounce words correctly and had particular difficulty with vowels, I ended up being a very "pore spelor."

When I asked how to spell a word, the teacher always told me to go look it up, with no other guidance. It would take me up to half an hour to find a word in a dictionary because I didn't pronounce it correctly in the first place. Since spelling and penmanship were the primary measures of evaluating writing skills in those days, I kept my sentences short and stuck to three-letter words whenever possible. Not a great beginning.

I bring up my background to point out the irony that, even though MFW has a degree in literature and I eked by with Cs and Ds in English, I was the one who taught our daughters to read. My take on this is that when you have struggled with a topic yourself, it is sometimes easier to empathize with the struggling student than if you are overly educated on a subject. (A further irony is that MFW fixes our computers even though I used to design computer digital circuits.)

With their preparation, practice with letters, being read to and told stories for years, they were ready to read—but on their terms (perhaps I nudged just a little).

Watching them, I realized their reading approach more closely resembled the breaking of codes than anything else. They progressed as follows.

Page 1, first word. "Tom."

So far the accumulation of D*'s entire reading knowledge is that all words are Tom, this one word being the entire population of their known reading vocabulary.

Page 2, second word. "Nancy."

OK. This becomes a bit more complicated but isn't too bad. All words that start with T are "Tom" and all words that start with N are "Nancy." Since both N and T are familiar letters, this division of D*'s reading space into two distinct vocabulary areas, "Tom" and "Nancy," is quite doable with minimal difficulty.

Page 3, "and." Oops, a lowercase letter. Since we introduced lowercase letters along with the caps, this is only a small speed bump. It is true that she was more familiar with uppercase letters but, since her new reading space has been expanded into only three regions, "Tom," "Nancy," plus "and," absorbing this third word is manageable.

Page 4, "Tom and Nancy." Her first combination and reinforcement of what she had already learned.

Page 5. "Pat," the dog. (Whatever happened to Spot?)

Pat's introduction, i.e., "P," forced her word-space to be expanded into four regions instead of three regions.

Her next real challenge didn't come until she encountered two words that began with the same letter. She then had to decide how to differentiate between these two. Both D4 and D5 used the second letter in the word to differentiate between these two words so they had to reach for new skills to extend their reading vocabulary. If they had instead opted for word length as the differentiator, I would have stepped in to steer them back to using the second letter.

I was not really a reading teacher but rather a guide who kept them from straying too far off track. I turned the pages, got the snacks, and helped with hints when asked, but spent most of my time in awe watching them break the code and absorb each new word into their known read-space.

D4 read her first book (with sixteen unique words) in one afternoon and became so excited that she had to immediately call her grandmother and read to her over the phone. Then she had to read it to her older sister in Colorado and to any of our guests who happened to drop by during the next few days. I have never seen any one before or since this accomplishment so proud of herself.

MFW was equally successful in working with them in music, art, and typing (probably the most important skill ever).

Not everything ended up with a successful outcome, however. When it came to teaching them how to clean their rooms or how to address me as "most intelligent and wonderful father," I completely bombed out.

You Can't Do That!

MFW was not pleased with me for defacing library property. I didn't think of my actions so much as marking up library books as instigating a convenient form of personal bookkeeping.

While in first grade D5 was on a roll when it came to devouring books. Although this was partly motivated by her teacher's setting an overall class goal of 3,500 books read by year's end, her main drive came from her love of exercising her new found reading power. D5 and I would go to the Children's Library almost daily to return and check out her reading fodder. She would typically finish two or three books by the time we reached home. During my runs to the library without her, I discovered I couldn't remember which books she had read and which were still fair game.

Solution: I took to marking the upper right corner of the inside flap of every book she had read with a dot. MFW was not pleased but this marking was the only way I could keep track of the available inventory. By early May it became almost impossible to find an unmarked book.

Now that the statute of limitations has run out, I feel safe about confessing to this serious breach of the library rules. D5's teacher did exceed her goal that year but largely due to D5's reading over 1,000 of those books. Fifteen years after the fact, I revisited this same library and discovered a good fifth of the children's books on the shelf still marked with our telltale dots.

*When an eighth grader is making her high school
choice, she does not appreciate the fact that a
month into ninth grade, she will most likely have
a completely new set of friends.*

5 3
VALUE OF FRIENDSHIP

D4 and S were good friends in the eighth grade and would often hang out together during recess.

The phone rings. It is S.

"D4, how are you doing on our English homework for tomorrow?"

"I'm finished, S."

"I always have trouble with the poetry assignments and you are so good at them. How long did it take you?"

"About an hour. Do you want me to read it to you?"

"I'd love to hear it. Go ahead."

"On a day when even rainbows..."

"That was beautiful. Can I hear it again? But read it more slowly."

"Sure. On a day when..."

Next day in class.

"OK, class. Get your poems out. S, you haven't read for a long time. Could you read your poem for the class?"

"OK. 'On a day when even rainbows...'"

"Very good, S. You have really improved."

"Now D4, could you read your poem?"

D4 was horrified. S had stolen her poem and read it in class as her own. D4 made up one on the spot, but it wasn't very good. S received her first A, D4 her first C. The friendship was over. S never apologized. D4 never mentioned it to S and never spoke to her again. S sold her friendship so cheaply and lost so much more than she had gained. Did she learn from her transgression? I have no idea but the odds are against it. Few understand that we are responsible for most of our own luck.

In high school D5 was sold down the river more than once by self-promoting classmates and, although painful, it did teach her to establish her own integrity standards for herself and her friends.

It's An Easy Test

True, friendship should never need testing. But in the real world, it's always nice to know. For this reason I explained life's rules #9 and #10 to my daughters (see chapter 60).

Rule #9: If a friend requests a temporary loan of a few dollars ($5 for example), always lend it. After all, a credit check can run $25 dollars. Learning who you can trust by risking a mere $5 is a good deal.

Rule #10: If you find it necessary to borrow a few bucks from a friend, always pay it back as soon as possible—see rule #9.

*A thief never robs a house with five daughters.
No money, too dangerous (hazards), and
too much toxic waste.*

5 4

MINI-MEANS

MINI-MEAN I

I inadvertently dropped a large ice cube onto the napkin on my lap at an upscale restaurant. My philosophy has always been to look for the opportunity offered by a new event rather than view it as a problem.

"D4. Spit out that little ice cube you're sucking and let me see if I can make it bigger for you."

She had a very doubtful look on her face but, as there wasn't anything else going on until the food arrived, she complied and spit it into my hand.

I covered the small ice cube with my other hand and, while employing a small diversion tactic, dropped her ice cube on the floor under the table where it wouldn't be noticed and replaced it with the larger one from my napkin.

Then the performance began.

"If you squeeze it really hard with both hands like this and blow on the end of your hand to get the cooling effect like this, sometimes the ice cube will grow. Umm. Aghh. Uhuh. There. Let's see what we've got."

"Wow! How did you do that?"

"It's a trick I learned while staying with some Marshallese friends on a small remote island near the equator in the middle of the Pacific Ocean."

"Will you teach me how to do that? Please?"

"Not until you're ten. That will give you a few years to see if you can figure it out for yourself."

"Pleeeeeese. Do it again!"

"This trick is so difficult and takes so much psychic energy that I can only do it once a night."

I repeated the trick for her and her friends numerous times over the next few years. Then a month before she turned ten, she had the epiphany. Ding, ding. The little bell went off in her head.

"I can't believe I let you fool me for all that time."

"You always knew you had a mean Daddy."

MINI-MEAN II

Every weekday at 5:25 p.m., I would get off the plane and ride my bike home to where my horde of small pints was waiting for me at around 5:40 p.m. Since dinner was a good hour away and there was no TV on the island, the gang of six (actually it varied between four and eight including my three) was pretty happy to have someone to play with if just to break up their boredom.

We'd start by making a string of seven across the road (there were very few cars on the island) and sing, "Do, Re, Mi" from *Sound of Music*. When we got to "Fa, a long, long way to run," we'd take off running down the road. There was a bus stop two blocks from our home where we would end up congregating at the end of our singing/running adventure.

The bus stop was enclosed on three sides and open on the fourth. The sturdy roof provided shelter even during the strong downpours so common during the rainy season (I think the record one-day total accumulation on one of these islands was twenty-eight inches).

"OK. Let's play hide and seek. I'll hide, and you all try to find me. I promise I will not cross either of those two roads, that fence over there or that driveway. OK?"

"OK." "Sure." "Yes" "Uh-huh." "I have to go to the bathroom."

Ten minutes after potty stop #6, we started anew.

"You stay right here and count to ten. No cheating—keep your eyes closed."

"1, 2, 3..."

I had them count in front of the open side while I slid around to the backside and quietly climbed up the wall and settled in for a two-minute nap atop the shelter.

My wards checked behind the few trees in the vicinity and then circled and circled the shelter totally clueless. Eventually the entire gang would congregate in front of the open side to go over what could possibly be wrong with their strategy.

I would take this opportunity to climb down off the roof and announce loudly as I rounded the open side, "How come you didn't find me?

They never discovered my secret. I'm so mean.

MINI-MEAN III

"Look D4, there's Mommy in her car ahead of us."

"Oh yeah. I think it's her. It's her car all right. But I can't quite see. Can you get a little closer?

For the next ten minutes I would close in on the target car to the point D4 could almost make out the identity of the driver, whose appearance was close to her mother's, then back off.

Finally I had to point out to D4 that we were in her mother's car and that meant the other car couldn't have been hers.

I'm mean. I'm mean. I'm just plain rotten.

MINI-MEAN IV

For the better part of a day, while driving from Minnesota to Colorado, I had D1, D2, and D3 convinced cows had flat noses because their heads were so heavy that they had to rest them on the ground most of the time. Finally D1, eight at the time, figured out that the cows were grazing and not resting.

Mean, mean, mean.

Grown children seem to be so much smarter these days. I never hear them threatening to run away from home anymore. Now it's the parents who are threatening to leave.

5 5

Panther Tracts VII

AWOL ON AOL

Parent (to pre-Misk), "Oops, you forgot your spelling list. Oh well, you can have Alan fax it to you."

"Oh, Daddy, nobody uses faxes anymore. That's last year stuff. I'll just have Tif email me a copy."

I can't keep up! I have three engineering degrees, eleven years of college, several years of teaching math and engineering, and I'm finding that I am struggling to keep up with yesterday's technology while my Misk and pre-Misk are navigating the info superhighway with abandonment. There's just no way. I'm strongly considering strategic surrender. No wonder the common dream of the multi-daughtered father is to live in the remote mountains or on a deserted beach.

Fast forward: The above paragraphs were written in 1995 when email was new. We've evolved through text messaging, IMing, YouTube, and Facebook since then, making the rest of this article dated so I've eliminated it. I can just imagine how my parents would had addressed this subject sixty-five years ago—writing on paper versus using a manual electric typewriter.

Human nature evolves over millennia whereas technology in the hands of teenagers evolves over weeks.

Misk Really Is AWOL Ghostwritten by father

My favorite Misk really was AWOL on this, our last *Panther Tracks* contribution. Her response (or more appropriately, her rebuttal) was never written so I had to go it alone. Of course the readership fell off as her writing talents and observations were more poignant, more erudite, better written, and more entertaining than mine while hitting an empathetic note with her peers.

She begged off, citing her heavy surge in homework and extracurricular activities, none of which I bought. Having gone through this before with her older sisters and taking into account that she had just turned fourteen, I realized there were two reasons for her resigning from this project.

The first reason: I was demoted, a common occurrence beginning when a daughter approaches her fourteenth birthday. At about twelve, she began to consider me an annoyance—friendly but clueless. At fourteen she demoted me from a minor adversary to a nonentity—not worth talking about, thinking about, or dealing with. Poof, I had become invisible.

The second reason: boys.

This turn in events is both a loss and a gain. I lose a valuable writing colleague but gain the opportunity of becoming her ghostwriter (with a vested interest). I'm sure if she had responded, it would have been something along these lines:

"My parents are so wonderful and so smart. I look forward to keeping them up to date on my day-to-day activities and seek their counsel when anything disturbs me. I do appreciate their chaperoning me, their setting such reasonable rules and guidelines for me such as my curfew, who I can have as friends, and how long I can remain on the phone. I know this is all for my own good—they are so wise."

I may have biased this ghostwriting a tiny, tiny bit but since it didn't get published in the *Panther Tracks*, it never mattered. OK, perhaps I did wait for twelve years before showing it to her and even then her only response was the famous daughter-eye-rolling maneuver. Parents need a fantasy now and then, too.

Signed Misk's Ghostwriter

D4, it's fine if you want to be a vegetarian, but that does mean you will have to start eating vegetables. As far as I know, there are no such things as an ice-cream-etarians (or M&M-etarians).

56

YOU EMBARRASSED ME!

"You embarrassed me."

"Sure looks like you're not happy with me. I'm sorry, D5, that I did this to you, but I'm not sure what I did."

"My friend A slept over last night."

"Is that how I embarrassed you?"

"Nooo. She asked me what time it was."

"I can't quite see how that would embarrass a sixth grader, for I'm sure we taught you how to read a clock—especially a digital one."

"That's not what I mean."

"Sorry. Please go on."

"I glanced at the clock and said 'It's 2 to the 10th.'"

"I see. And what happened then?"

"She stared at me and then said, '**What on earth are you talking about?**'"

"I never said you would grow up normal. These things are bound to happen."

Explanation: When I was teaching D5 and her friends Ping-Pong, I would make them start with "2" and have them double its value every time they returned the ball. So they would eventually count 2, 4, 8, 16, 32, 64, 128, 256, 512, 1,024...routinely without thinking about it, assuming they made a successful return of course. I emphasized the fact that "2 to the 6th" equals 64 and more importantly, "2 to the 10th equals 1,024".

"Look. The value of 2 to the 6th starts with a 6 and the value of 2 to the 10th starts with a 10. These are the only examples where the power and the beginning of the value are the same. If you remember these two powers of 2, you can figure out the rest on the fly."

D5 grew up assuming that not only did all kids know their powers of two but, like the multiplication tables, knew them so well that their values were virtually a working part of their vocabulary. So when she observed that the clock indicated 10:24 p.m., she automatically responded, "It's 2 to the 10th" without a second thought.

I further taught them that 2 to the 10th equaling 1,024, can be approximated by 1,000. Since the symbol k (for kilo) is used to represent 1,000, then 2 to the 10th is essentially 1k. Similarly, since (2 to the 10th) × (2 to the 10th) equals (2 to the 20th) or approximately 1,000,000, 2 to the 20th can be represented by 1m (pronounced "meg"). This introduction to the powers of two gave the Ds an early understanding of the origin of such terms as kilobytes and megabits of memory and corresponding data rate specifications. In the world of computers and communication, our thinking has evolved from a linear world to a logarithmic world.

Exiting the London tube one hears, "Mind the
Gap," my companion explains this refers to the
gap between the train's doorway and the platform.
As a father of daughters, I know better. They are
warning me about the generation gap.

57

DADDY MATH III

AS THEY GET OLDER

Family dynamics eventually reduce the effectiveness of teaching your own children. We are no exception. Ds learned what parental buttons to push when they don't want parental help. They really became quite creative at twisting any situation to their favor.

Partly for this reason and partly because we saw real growth opportunities, we enrolled D4 and D5 in various extracurricular math programs including Kumon (developed by Mr. Toru Kumon in Japan) and EPGY (Stanford's Education Program for Gifted Youth) between second and seventh grades. Kumon, with its emphasis on speed, is to math as typing is to writing. It is not necessary to be a good typist to be a good writer, but it sure helps. They stuck with it for a few years until competing interests, particularly music, sports, sleepovers and being a teenager encroached on their discretionary time.

Our poor daughters did not get a reprieve during our ten-week summer vacation to Alaska. Since I had taken the Kumon instructor training to stay abreast of their progress, I had copies of all the Kumon worksheets. Each day of our trip, even the day we crossed the Arctic Circle in the Yukon (just after MFW gave them each a half-hour piano lesson), both daughters were treated to thirty minutes of Kumon practice. Parents can be so mean sometimes.

My call to Kumon in those days was: "Kumon. Kum-on over here. It's time for your math."

While we were evaluating middle schools for D5 we conferred with the sixth grade public school advisor who, after learning D5 had completed Algebra I and half of Algebra II through EPGY, agreed with us that her taking sixth grade math would be a complete waste.

A week later the advisor got back to us with the news that, in the eyes of the State of California, if D5 did not take sixth-grade math as part of their school curriculum, she would not be properly educated. Option denied. Even the advisor thought this was dumb.

As a result we switched her to a private school that, after a thorough evaluation, started her in seventh-grade math and subsequently promoted her to eighth grade algebra midyear, enabling her to complete AP calculus by her sophomore year.

DOWNSIDE OF BEING AHEAD

Except for senior English, D5 had all the credits needed to graduate high school and expressed an interested in applying to college a year early.

We contacted the NCAA to assure she would be eligible to compete in her sport in college. The NCAA representative I conferred with informed us that, if she had sufficient credits except for senior English, had a minimum SAT-grade score and at least two years of math (she had six), one of which had to be Algebra I, she would be eligible to compete in college sports.

Then he added, the NCAA would not allow any course taken before ninth grade to be counted toward her eligibility.

I explained that she had completed Algebra I, Algebra II and Trig all before ninth grade.

"Then she she's not eligible."

I argued with the NCAA representative for twenty minutes that, since she had earned an A in AP calculus in tenth grade, she was certainly not deficient in math."

"Doesn't matter. The rules are the rules."

That's when I realized the NCAA representatives' only interest was to protect themselves and not help the athletes they were supposed to represent, unfortunately not an uncommon problem.

Rules implemented to prevent great athletes but weak students from being drafted from high school before they were academically prepared were being interpreted to hurt high achievers for whom high school had nothing further to offer.

"D5, you have enough wiggle space in your schedule. Do you just want to add senior English to your schedule and graduate a year early to avoid the NCAA eligibility problem?"

"Yeah."

"Done."

She made NCAA Academic All-American her freshman year.

*Scientists have determined that the reason fathers
with five daughters can swim so far underwater
is because they spend so much of their life holding
their breath.*

5 8

SWIMMING

I found myself cringing while I watched the young father try to teach his daughter how to swim.

"Now blow out when your face is under the water. That way, the bubbles will act like a jet engine and make you go faster."

His physics was shaky but ironically, he was really doing the right thing in helping his daughter learn to swim. He was playing with her, and she was having a great time just being in the water. You can't be a good swimmer unless you love the water, and the earlier you're exposed to it, the more you will learn to love it.

Even parents who are non-swimmers themselves can get their kids off on the right fin by just giving them "water time." The more time a tot spends in the water, the more she develops the instincts of how her body physically interacts with it.

Adults who never experienced being in the water as a child have been known to drown in water less than three feet deep because once they lose their balance, they lack the instincts needed to recover their footing. They also tend to panic when they feel pressure on their lungs, which an experienced swimmer isn't even aware of. Any child who has spent many hours just playing in a pool instinctively recovers her footing by pulling her hands in the opposite direction she wants her feet to go.

I started bringing all five daughters to the pool and the beach when they were only a few months old. OK, I admit I pushed D5 a little bit by giving her first swim lesson at a younger age than the other four. I was anxious to get started.

"MFW, D5 is not doing very well with her first swim lesson."

"What seems to be the problem?"

"She kicks with bent knees even though I'm showing her how to keep them straight."

"Is that all?"

"No, she keeps trying to do flip turns. This skill is too advanced for her right now. Maybe later."

"I think you're rushing things a tad."

"Do you think so?"

"Yes. She's only five minutes old. I'm sure when she's ten minutes old she'll do much better. After all, she will have doubled her age by then."

I started by having them lay on their backs in the pool and, supporting them with only a hand under their heads, towed them around the pool. If you blow into a baby's face, she will automatically hold her breath, enabling her to be dunked under the water with no effect other than a full laugh. By the time they were just short of a year, I could swim under water with them riding my back while they held onto my neck. They all thought this was normal.

We found it necessary to join a private swim club as the rules at public pools were too restrictive to do any fun stuff together, like walking around in chest deep water with them standing first on my shoulders then advancing to standing on my head without my supporting them in any manner. They loved diving for coins (not allowed at public pools), jumping to me off diving boards (not allowed), being thrown into the air...

Their favorite trick (a skill passed on from sister to sister, as they certainly didn't learn it from me) was to spend considerable effort trying to drown their favorite father in water five-feet deep. I'm still a bit worried remembering how they all laughed while trying to push me under. I'm alive; therefore, I survived (one more skill that I had to acquire in my world of daughters).

I swam competitively in both high school and college and taught swimming both during summer vacations in my youth and later as a bachelor on Kwajalein. As an engineer familiar with the physics involved, I was able to give my daughters an edge up in swimming proficiency. All five girls became excellent swimmers competing at the highest levels between six and sixteen.

It's my belief that if you can keep a daughter in competitive condition through maturation, they will never lose their love of physical activity, especially swimming. All five are still in excellent condition and swim whenever their schedules permit. I am happy to report that my eldest granddaughter is carrying on this tradition.

All the experts report that educating you kids will provide a good return. I didn't realize that they meant following graduation, your kids will return and move back in with you.

59

BEST HOUSE DESIGN FOR FIVE DAUGHTERS

I have several issues with existing home designs. In my opinion, many housing codes overreach their mandate of safety, efficiency, and preservation of neighborhood values and impinge on design features, thus handicapping innovation. Furthermore, during house-hunting forays, buyers will keep in mind future resale values. They know a home design that is too far from mainstream will appeal to a limited subset of homebuyers, hurting its potential for appreciation and easy resale. Builders are aware of this fact as well and build accordingly.

It is for the above reasons that the optimum home design for a household of two parents and five daughters with limited financial resources (a given with five daughters) will probably never be built. It is my opinion that a home designed to provide maximum harmony and learning opportunities with cost constraints should, at a minimum, be designed to have:

1) Six and a half bathrooms

2) Two bedrooms

3) Nine big closets (D4 made me add "big")

4) The biggest kitchen possible, and

5) A music/project room containing a large guest bed (for the inevitable sleepovers).

While working overseas at a missile test site, I once babysat for a family with five daughters (giving me a preview of what was to come) sardined into a small two-bedroom half-duplex (housing was at a premium). The five daughters had adjusted to the crammed conditions by removing all the furniture from their shared bedroom except two sets of drawers and five mattresses, which they pushed together on the floor. Even after disposing of the bed frames, the five mattresses and two sets of drawers took up eighty percent of the floor area. Yet the girls made do, which proved to me that it really is possible for five daughters to share one bedroom.

My minimum design would have one bedroom for the parents and one for the daughters.

When our family moved to our present house, D5 and D4 each gained possession of their own private bathrooms. This improvement ushered in a new era of peace and tranquility with their domestic conflicts subsiding by at least seventy percent. Daughters can handle sharing bedrooms (just look at all the sleepovers), but bathrooms can become fierce territorial battlefields. This is a subject most fathers can't begin to understand so avoid thinking about it. Girls are very protective where bathroom real estate is concerned and are particularly sensitive about protecting their allocated space and personal possessions.

"Did you use my hairbrush again?"

"Of course not. You've got cooties."

"Why is my towel wet?"

"I cleaned the toilet with it. [Smirk.] All right, I didn't actually use it on the toilet. You left it on the floor and after you took a shower—it got wet. Don't worry. I would never use your towel to clean the toilet. I used your toothbrush instead!"

"Mom!"

"Where are all the hair ties? I just bought a dozen new ones."

"They're in your drawer. I put them there 'cause you were leaving them on my side of the sink and all over the floor. By the way, you used up all my shampoo."

"There was hardly any left."

"Oh, like that's a good reason?"

Any parent with more than one daughter will confirm that I am downplaying my portrayal of what really transpires during daughter-to-daughter bathroom co-occupancy struggles.

I have no doubt that a good way to minimize "forbidden use" of personal items, to reduce the "unauthorized borrowing" of clothes, and to assure the happiness of the family is to design one's house so that each daughter's closet is accessible only through her private bathroom. There is no need for any sister to ever enter another's sacred bathroom (and thus have access to her closet) unless specifically invited—and preferably only with a written invitation in the form of a single-entry closet visa.

When daughters no longer share bathrooms, the risk of fights and physical injury is considerably reduced, along with the odds of parents suffering mental breakdowns.

The sixth bathroom is of course, allocated to the parents (OK, mostly to the mother unit) and the half bath as a guest bathroom (or as a default bathroom for the father unit when it's too cold to use the great outdoors).

After the first five closets are allocated to the daughters, three are allocated to the mother: two for her clothes and one large one for her inadequate shoe collection. A closet reserved for a woman's shoes has become the norm ever since Imelda Marcos set the standard thirty years ago.

The remaining closet is for the husband, albeit shared with luggage, Christmas decorations and winter coats.

All parents know that the kitchen is where the real living takes place. It provides the environment for more activities than all the remaining rooms in the house combined—including the project room.

The music/project/activity room is a no-brainer in our family. We have a grand piano, a parlor grand, three 1880s pump organs, two cellos, a trumpet, flute, two guitars, banjo, accordion, and bongo drums. Ongoing projects take on a life of their own and quickly spread throughout the kitchen and music room regardless of any attempt at containing them. We've succumbed to a pure surrender policy of letting the daughters and their projects do what they must.

I had the stewardess convinced that D1, tucked in a blanket with feet curled under, was under three and did not need a ticket. Then she poked her head out and asked, "Daddy, is this a 747 or a DC10?" (Shut up, kid!)

6 0

RULES OF LIFE

A father is never sure if he will live long enough to pass on his knowledge, his wisdom, or even his bad jokes to his children. Since many of life's lessons can be boiled down to a set of basic "Rules of Life," I have decided to summarize my version of these rules for the next generation. Children learn more readily from other adults than from their own parents, so perhaps my rules will be useful to the children of others and my children can learn a set of similar rules from other parents.

Here is a sampling of my rules of life for my favorite daughters.

Rule 1: Love your partner (MFW in my case).

Rule 2: See rule 1.

Rule 4a: If the wife isn't happy, the husband isn't happy.

Rule 4b: If the wife isn't happy, nobody's happy.

Rule 5: When in doubt about the important things in life, see rule 4.

Rule 9: Never ask small loans to be repaid. The value of this inherent credit report, i.e., did they repay the loan voluntarily or conveniently forget about it, is far more valuable than the pittance involved.

Rule 10: Religiously repay all small loans as quickly as possible (see rule 9).

Rule 14: Never steal anything unless a single theft is enough to live on for the rest of your life and the odds of getting caught are less the 1.6 percent (0.35 percent if you are risk averse).

Rule 17: If someone tries to convince you to eat an exotic meat dish with the persuasion, "Try it. You'll like it. It tastes like chicken.", don't eat it; eat chicken.

Rule 21: Don't insist on finding Mr. Right, for as D4/D5's godmother explains, his first name may be "Always."

Rule 22: The flavor is in the fat so forget about eating low-fat. Just eat less.

Rule 26: Never skip an opportunity to show your children you love them. Avoid platitudes and empty praises. It's bad form when a parent tells his daughter, "I knew you would do well," when he didn't bother to take the time to find out what she actually did.

Rule 31: If they use terms such as: zero defects, zero tolerance, leave no child behind, wipe out drugs, just say no, or war on ** (any social problem)—they are idiots, as any statistician or realist can tell you. For example, a "zero defect" program only encourages people to cover up problems, "zero tolerance" leads to unreasonable punishments, "leave no child behind" means the bus never leaves the station, "wipe out drugs" can be accomplished only by killing everyone, and "just say no" sounds good when addressing the mind but it's the heart that is in charge.

Rule 36: Ninety-five percent of the values you pass on to your children occurs in the first ten years of parenting. The rest is reinforcement (surprise, they actually hear more than you think).

Rule 38: If you maintain a high level of integrity (how you treat others), then you don't need to worry about ethics (someone else's code, which may or may not match your own) or morals (what you may do that affects no one).

Rule 39: If you are under thirty do not freak out your mother, it's not worth it.

Rule 41: In marriage follow the 60-60 rule. Each spouse should be prepared to carry 60 percent of the load. A 50-50 rule will produce interpretation conflicts, i.e., your 55 percent may look like 45 percent to me. (When the question is asked, "How often does the husband wash the dishes?" the husband may respond 35 percent of the time while the wife claims he washes the dishes only 15 percent of the time.)

Anything over 60 percent is unfair and reduces the productivity of the marriage.

Rule 43: Responding to a dare is giving power to your adversary. Nothing is dumber.

Rule 46: Compassion is not weakness. Being nice does not mean you are a wimp. Compromise, compromise, compromise, kill! You never need to draw the "do not cross line" in the sand more than three times before responding in a most forceful manner (enough is enough).

Rule 47: Remember the Great Wall of China was never breached from the outside the wall—the downfall came from within the wall. Our real danger is not from terrorists, invaders, or criminal states but from the self-righteous and those who "hide" behind the flag and God. Please note: I don't find fault with those who profess a strong belief in God and/or flag, only those who hide behind that belief (waving the flag and espousing a belief in God has been a successful political ploy throughout history).

Rule 49: It should be legal for any person over eighty-five to use any drugs they want (assuming they are not an active commercial pilot).

Rule 53: Don't let your daughters shy away from math. Math is power and after all, equality is based on power sharing.

Rule 54: Arithmetic is dumb. Math is fun. Arithmetic is to math as typing is to writing. It's not necessary to know how to type in order to be a good writer but it makes life so much simpler if you do.

Rule 58: When you are wrong, admit your mistake—especially to your children. They will learn to emulate you someday. Plus "perfect" parents fall the furthest when they make a mistake and are the hardest to forgive.

Rule 59: Listen, listen, ask, listen, listen, and talk in that order (this is the rule, which for me, has always been the most difficult to follow).

Rule 63: If someone advertises how much money you will save but doesn't tell you the price up front, don't bother—you can't afford it.

Rule 67: Only gamble when the expected loss is less than its entertainment value. I broke this rule the last time we were in Las Vegas. I just lost all control. It was so embarrassing. I set a $10 limit for my losses but on this particular outing, I exceeded my limit by 20 percent and lost $12.25 (the casinos hate me).

Rule 68: Everyone is interesting to listen to for fifteen minutes (D4 and D5's godmother claims that there are a few people from Ohio who don't make the fifteen-minute cut, but then she's from Ohio). Many are interesting for two hours, some are interesting for a whole weekend, but only a very few are interesting for a lifetime (I got lucky and married a lifer).

Rule 71: When you bring your wife her morning coffee in bed, make sure it is at the optimal temperature and she has a small towel to handle drips. For Trophy Husbands, the time limit between her uttering the magic word "coffee" and its appearance at her bedside is forty-five seconds. (See my next book, The Challenges of Being a Trophy Husband, for more details.)

Rule 73: Parents are happy if their children are happy and successful. Children are successful if they a) aren't involved in drugs, b) don't smoke, c) use their adverbs correctly, and d) have an above average love life. It's hard to beat family love.

Rule 74: There are two ways to get ahead financially: "make more" or "spend less." Doing both is even better.

Rule 76: When your wife brings you coffee in bed, make sure it is hot enough. If it is not, send it back (this is what I refer to as my fantasy rule).

Rule 78: When hailing a taxi, if it has no meter, look for another taxi.

Rule 81: When a daughter tells you how much money she is going to save you—**run!**

Rule 82: When your wife tells you how much she is saving you, cancel all planned capital expenditures.

Rule 86: Contrary to what MFW may say, RV does not stand for Ruined Vacation.

Rule 88: Keep your wife off balance with acts of random kindness (flowers for no reason except that you love her). She may protest that she doesn't want the attention—she wants the attention.

Rule 89: Be on a constant vigil for those very dangerous questions from your partner: i.e., "Does this dress make me look heavy?" or "Was your former girlfriend more...?"

Rule 91: When it comes to a technical question about your house, an appliance, your car, the source of intergalactic gamma rays or an investment, three degrees from MIT and a week of research are no match for a casual opinion from a wife's girlfriend.

Rule 92: Investigate all noises late at night even if you know their exact cause. It shows your wife you love her, which is all she really cares about anyway.

Rule 93: Life is too serious to take seriously.

Rule 96: Never get so overconfident that you believe your own resume.

Rule 97: Never adjust spending to match your financial statement. It's a lie anyway.

Rule 98a: Go before you go,

Rule 98b: Pee before you flee,

Rule 98c: Take a leak before you seek,

Rule 98d: When in doubt, empty out! (My favorite)

Rule 98e: Pee to the lee (for the nautical readers).

Rule 99: Don't worry about treating your children equally. Treating them fairly is all that matters.

Rule 100: If a caller won't tell you what city they are calling from "for security reasons," explain to them, "I'm sorry but we are not allowed to accept calls from undisclosed locations for security reasons."

Time Rules

Thirty-Eight Seconds: If you can't find your dog's "Do your biz" in thirty-eight seconds, it never happened.

Thirty-Nine Seconds: The length of time an unsolicited caller has to actually tell you what he or she wants. Lengthy inquiries as to your health are a sign to hang up.

Forty-Five Seconds: If you can't find the interest rate they are actually going to charge you within forty-five seconds because they hide it in pages and pages of explanations of how much you are going to save or how you can spend the money, pitch it. (Do they really think I don't know how to spend money? It's easy. All I have to do is to ask any one of my daughters to help.)

Four days: Time to call your mother.

Thirty-eight years: Get the daughter off the payroll.

Problem with bad memory on allowance day:
"OK. Next! Wait a minute—are you sure
you're one of my daughters?"
"Oh yes, Daddy. Don't you remember me?"
"Well OK. Next! Wait! You already
came through the line."
"Oh no, Daddy. You are getting forgetful."
Conundrum: If I only have five daughters,
why do I pay out twelve allowances?

6 1

UNIVERSAL LANGUAGE

Trying to communicate while traveling in a foreign country can be very exhausting, especially if the traveler lacks language skills to the extent that I do. My ears are always inadvertently on the alert for English or even something that resembles English. I can walk through the streets of a foreign city all day enjoying the sights but communication deprived.

Then it happens. Someone laughs. My head turns automatically toward the person laughing as I instinctively think, "Ah ha, English!"

Fortunately, there are some gestures a traveler can make that are understood by nearly anyone, for they are based on universal human needs. On the following page are four universal gestures a visitor might make to a local inhabitant in nearly any country where the local inhabitant would immediately grasp the visitor's meaning. The reader's job is to guess which of the following four responses listed below correspond to the depicted gestures.

A) Oh, I see you are sleepy and need a hotel.

B) Oh, I see you need the loo (WC, toilet, etc.).

C) Oh, I see you are hungry and need a restaurant.

D) Oh, I see you have daughters and therefore are in great need of vast amounts of money.

Gesture 1

Gesture 2

Gesture 3

Gesture 4

Understanding daughters is like trying to dig a hole all the way to China. Getting started is easy but getting there—no way!

6 2

APPLICATION TO DATE MY DAUGHTER

The problem with "Daughter Dating Applications" is one size does not fit all. The following four candidate application forms were designed to cover most of a father's needs when choosing an age-appropriate application form to give to a would-be suitor.

General Guidelines Versus Age

Form	Age range	Motivation
A	Up to 15.8 years	Hide Daughter
B	15.8 years to 18 years	Protect Daughter
C	18 years to 25 years	Worry about Daughter
D	Over 25	Get Grandchildren

Application To Date My Daughter: A

Dear Applicant,

No way!!!!

You may reapply when my daughter turns sixteen provided you continue to lead an exemplary life. We take no responsibility for your emotional and physical well-being should you give my daughter too much attention before then.

As an informational footnote, we feel it is only fair to inform the applicant that the father has fourth-degree black belts in two separate martial arts, the mother has an Olympic bronze medal for pistol, and the uncle is an assistant to the director of the CIA heading the interrogation division. In addition, we have dinner every Sunday with our dear and close family friend, the Chief of Police.

APPLICATION TO DATE MY DAUGHTER: B

This application is incomplete unless accompanied by notarized copies of applicant's transcripts, SAT scores, driving record and 3 letters of reference. If accepted, applicant will be notified to make appointments for physical and psychiatric exams and in-depth interviews.

Full Name _____DOB____GPA _____

SS#_____ Blood Type _____ DL# _____

Address _____ How Long _____

Sat/AP scores V___ M ___ II ___ Boy Scout Rank____

Note: You need not apply if you 1) have a water bed or a truck with a gun rack, 2) use drugs or smoke, 3) have been arrested, 4) had a moving violation since 17, 5) have been suspended from school, 6) wear pants more than 3 inches off your hips, have a visible tattoo or sport piercing hardware, 7) have trouble using adverbs correctly (there will be a test).

If you have ever received a C or less since 8th grade, please attach detailed explanation.

Answer the following questions in 100 words or less.
A. What does "Don't be late" mean?
B. What does "abstinence" mean?
C. What does "**Don't touch my daughter**" mean?
D. What form of bodily harm do you fear most?
E. Are you willing to take a lie detector test?

I hereby swear the above is accurate under penalty of serious unpleasantness and possible severe damage to vital body parts.

Signed _____ Date _____

We feel it is only fair to inform the applicant that the father has 4th degree black belts, the mother an Olympic bronze medal for pistol, and the uncle is the director of the CIA's interrogation division.

APPLICATION TO DATE MY DAUGHTER: C

This application is incomplete unless accompanied by copies of applicant's transcripts, driving record, financial statements and 2 letters of reference. If accepted, applicant will be notified to make appointments for a psychiatric exam and family interview.

Name _____DOB_____SS#_____

Address _____ How Long _____

Blood Type ___ GPA_____ DL# _____

Note: You need not apply if you 1) use drugs, 2) have been arrested, 3) smoke, 4) did not graduate from high school, 5) have trouble using your adverbs correctly (there will be a test) or 6) don't have a job paying above minimum wage or aren't in college.

Answer the following questions in 100 words or less.

A. What form of bodily harm do you fear most?
B. Are you willing to take a lie detector test?
C. What is the best way not to anger an over-protective father?

Favorable answers to the following 4 questions will give you extra points and speed up your application process.

How do you feel about:

D. Buying your in-laws very expensive presents?
E. Taking in-laws on very expensive trips?
F. Paying education expenses for your wife?
G. Worrying about parent's retirement comfort?

I hereby swear the above is accurate under penalty of possible serious unpleasantness.

Signed _____ Date _____

APPLICATION TO DATE MY DAUGHTER: D

Name _____

Address* _____

Note: You need not apply if you 1) use drugs, 2) smoke, 3) can't support yourself or 4) are abusive.

Please answer following question in one word:

Do you have a pulse? _____

Be forewarned, by signing below the applicant hereby acknowledges that he does not hold the parents liable for any consequences he may encounter due to his associating with the daughter, such as severe disorientation, mental or physical duress, or extreme strain to his financial wellbeing.

Signed* _____

Unless you hear otherwise, this applicant is pre-approved.

*Optional

Note: Do not be alarmed if when you return from your third date, you discover the parents have rented their home and moved to Australia with no forwarding address. Should this event occur, we would first deposit $20,000 into our daughter's account to help defray her next year's living expenses.

*"I would have died sooner but, with so many
daughters, I was just too busy!"*

63

Another daydream

OBITUARY

Wait, wait, wait to get a word in.

Talk, talk, talk. Drone, drone, drone, drone...

Ever wonder what you would like your obituary to say?

Hmm...

Lynn A. Jacobson, 97, a retired engineer and successful author residing in Palo Alto since 1977, and his favorite wife, were passengers on the suspicious chartered "Party People Plane" (carrying several cases of the finest Champagne and no luggage) that flew into a Colorado mountain, Oct. 17, 2034. Mr. Jacobson is survived by 5 daughters, 25 grandchildren, 125 great-granddaughters, and 5 great-great granddaughters (plus 25 wannabes).

He was born in 1937 in Spokane, Washington, at a Salvation Army Home for unwed mothers, adopted and raised in Minnesota, educated in Massachusetts and worked in Colorado, California and the Marshall Islands.

Mr. Jacobson's best sellers include: *Surviving Five Daughters, Challenges of Being a Trophy Husband*, the popular *Bear Goo* children's series, *Remarkable Unremarkable People, Investing Secrets for My Children*, and his most recent super best seller, *If You're Over 72 and Not Having Fun, You're Doing It Wrong.*

Mr. Jacobson has left instructions that his ashes be divided among his 125 great-granddaughters to be scattered any place on earth they might choose. They are each to be provided with a three-month travel stipend for this purpose by his estate.

He has further instructed that his marker be placed on the family's Colorado mountain property. It is to be inscribed:

"If you have loved, been loved, lived with integrity and contributed more to the great jam jar of life than you took out, you have lived well."

"Daughter. After considerable thought we rewrote our wills based on three considerations."
"Oh, OK."
"One, we love you more than anything in the world. Two, children's lives can be ruined if they inherit too much money. And three, combining one and two..."
"Wait—wait a minute—it's OK! I'm willing to take that chance."
"No. We're sorry. We just can't take the risk of making your life miserable."

64

DAUGHTERS' REACTION

When D1–D5 were asked to comment on this collection of essays, they all gave virtually the same answer: "We tried to train our daddy for the last thirty years but, with only five of us contributing, we found we were grossly understaffed. He's barely trainable. Housebroken, yes—trainable, no.

"We are seriously considering writing our own book to tell our side of the story called, *Surviving One Daddy*. In it, we will lay out the futile efforts we employed to bring our father to within the realm of normalcy. The best progress we can report is that, under supervision, he can occasionally be let out into public for short intervals but only after dark."

GLOSSARY

E/T Estrogen/Testosterone ratio in a given household

E/T equal 1	Normal (or at least average)
E/T 2 or 3	Manageable but not easy
E/T 4 or 5	Survivable by only the very strong
E/T over 5	Requires serious intervention plus eligible for disabled placard

ET	Estrogen Tsunami
D1–D5	D1–D5 Daughter designation by birth order
HM	Hover Mother (definition obvious)
LBH	Line up By Height. A technique used to organize teens and preteens by height ostensibly to allow teams to be picked fairly from a mixed group. Real purpose is to allow organizer to stall while he figures out what to do next.
MDF	Multi-Daughtered Fathers
MFG	My Favorite Girlfriend
MFW	My Favorite Wife
PDF	Pente-Daughtered Father
PDSS	Post-Daughter Stress Syndrome (some multi-daughtered fathers claim that PDSS actually stands for Pre-Daughter Stress Syndrome, Present-Daughter Stress Syndrome, Post Daughter Stress Syndrome, and Permanent Daughter Stress Syndrome)

PDSSRP   84-step Post Daughter Stress Syndrome Recovery
            Program (under development)

WMD   Weapon of Macho Demise (dirty diaper)

Made in the USA